Virtual Worlds and Criminality

Kai Cornelius • Dieter Hermann
Editors

Virtual Worlds and Criminality

Springer

Editors
Dr. Kai Cornelius, LL.M.
Institute for German European and
International Criminal Law
University of Heidelberg
Friedrich-Ebert-Anlage 6-10
69117 Heidelberg
Germany
cornelius@jurs.uni-heidelberg.de

Prof. Dr. Dieter Hermann
Institute of Criminology
University of Heidelberg
Friedrich-Ebert-Anlage 6-10
69117 Heidelberg
Germany
hermann@krimi.uni-heidelberg.de

ISBN 978-3-642-20822-5 e-ISBN 978-3-642-20823-2
DOI 10.1007/978-3-642-20823-2
Springer Heidelberg Dordrecht London New York

Library of Congress Control Number: 2011933553

Printed on acid-free paper

Springer is part of Springer Science+Business Media (www.springer.com)

Preface

The fusion between virtuality and reality has achieved a new quality of experience by the establishment of metaverses and virtual worlds. With globally registered accounts nearing 800 million and revenues approaching US$ 1 billion annually (according to the Consulting Company *KZERO)*, virtual worlds such as *Second Life, Twinity, Entropia Universe,* or *Fregger* have experienced rapid growth in recent years and show no signs of slowing down. Not only have countless companies discovered these "virtureal worlds" as marketplaces, but also have fraudsters and other criminals.

The term *metaverse* is used herein to mean a social virtual world such as *Second Life, There,* or *Playstation Home.* It describes a permanently existing 3D virtual world close to reality in appearance, created by its participants and constantly evolving through their activities. The users have an "avatar" as the digital representation of their physical selves. They accomplish various goals: meeting and socializing with other avatars, buying and selling virtual items, playing games, and creating and decorating virtual homes and properties. Certain transactions among users result in a circular flow of real-world money, which takes place partly within the virtual world but are linked directly with the outside world via exchange rates.

Various Massively Multiplayer Online-Games (MMOGs) such as *Entropia Universe* and *World of Warcraft* contain elements that bear a resemblance to aspects of the metaverse, although the MMOGs typically focus on a specific gaming activity rather than on general-purpose socializing. These MMOGs are included in the more comprehensive concept of "virtual worlds".

To meet the new challenges arising from virtual worlds, the *Institute of German, European and International Criminal Law,* supported by the *Institute of Criminology,* both part of the *University of Heidelberg,* organized the symposium "Virtual Worlds and Criminality" at the *Internationales Wissenschaftsforum Heidelberg,* a center for scholarly exchange in all areas of science and academic research. This conference brought together European experts from different academic disciplines, *inter alia* representatives from jurisprudence, social sciences and media sciences, as well as from psychology. They discussed the reasons for and the impacts of these new forms of criminality as well as the necessities and possibilities for fighting these. Moreover, other fundamental issues were examined, such as the addictive potential of virtual-world use, media violence, and conflict resolution problems arising in the context of virtual worlds. These proceedings (which were made following the conference) provide insight into much of the results of the discussion.

The conference could not have taken place without the generous sponsorship of the *Deutsche Forschungsgemeinschaft,* Germany's largest research funding organization, and the inclusion of the conference in the symposia program by the curators' board of the *Internationales Wissenschaftsforum Heidelberg.*

The symposium and the publication of its proceedings would not have been possible without the help and cooperation of many members of the Institutes' staff. At the risk of overlooking important contributions of others, special mention should be made of Ms. *Julia Neugebauer* who coordinated administrative tasks and of Ms. *Johanna Nieswandt*, who assured the efficiency of the publication process.

Heidelberg, January 2011

Kai Cornelius
Dieter Hermann

Contents

Contributors

Kai Cornelius Institute for German, European and International Criminal Law, University of Heidelberg, Heidelberg, Germany, Cornelius@jurs.uni-heidelberg.de

Tilo Hartmann Department of Communication Science, Vrije Universiteit Amsterdam, Amsterdam, The Netherlands, t.hartmann@fsw.vu.nl

Dieter Hermann Institute of Criminology, University of Heidelberg, Heidelberg, Germany, hermann@krimi.uni-heidelberg.de

Christoph Klimmt Department of Journalism and Communication Research, Hanover University of Music, Drama and Media, Hannover, Germany, christoph.klimmt@ijk.hmtm-hannover.de

Christian Laue Institute of Criminology, University of Heidelberg, Heidelberg, Germany, laue@krimi.uni-heidelberg.de

Arno R. Lodder Department Transnational Legal Studies, Computer/Law Institute, Vrije Universiteit Amsterdam, Amsterdam, The Netherlands, a.r.lodder@vu.nl

Bert Theodor teWildt Centre for Psychological Medicine, Hannover Medical School, Hannover, Germany, tewildt.bert@mh-hannover.de

Virtual Worlds as a Regulatory Challenge: A User Perspective

Christoph Klimmt

Abstract Multi-User Environments offer a broad range of possibilities to experience action-oriented contexts, for example, simulations of real-world contexts, materializations of fictional contexts (e.g., the "Lord of the Rings" universe), and the co-creation of mixed virtual–real interaction spaces such as "Second Life". The chapter elaborates the key elements of multi-user environments from a user perspective: Interactivity, mediated interpersonal communication, easy accessibility, and reflects on the motivational appeal of these characteristics. From this reconstruction of what multi-user environments "can do", implications for effects perspectives are derived, such as the diffusion of responsibility and liability for events and actions (including potentially illegal actions) occurring in multi-user environments. The chapter builds on these considerations to point out effect issues of scientific interest, most importantly, new dimensions of copyright issues and transfer effects (stimulation or facilitation of real-world crime by virtual multi-user environments). Finally, conceptually most central themes for interdisciplinary research on legal/criminal effects of multi-user environments are discussed, namely "sense of right and wrong" in virtual versus real contexts, media literacy and prevention of transfer effects, and the legal status of virtual spaces and the actions conducted in them.

1 Introduction

Virtual multi-user environments or "Metaverses" have evolved to a major challenge for academic research of various disciplines, including communication, psychology, law, and criminology. The relevance of this attention for virtual worlds is justified by two major developments: (1) A large and still growing number of people who

C. Klimmt (✉)
Department of Journalism and Communication Research, Hanover University of Music, Drama, and Media, Hannover, Germany
e-mail: christoph.klimmt@ijk.hmtm-hannover.de

K. Cornelius and D. Hermann (eds.), *Virtual Worlds and Criminality*,
DOI 10.1007/978-3-642-20823-2_1,

attend virtual worlds, for example, for play, social interaction, and/or work, and (2) rapid advancement of the technical capabilities that allow for ever-new possibilities in terms of use and commercial exploitation. Virtual Worlds (VWs) are clearly on their way to occupy an important and distinct meaning in everyday life of tomorrow. With those VWs that are currently available rising many questions, including liability issues, legal regulation, and criminal prosecution (see the various chapters in this volume), it is important to reflect proactively about "what's in VWs" that renders them so appealing to users and producers alike. Understanding the power of VWs early in their evolution should allow to take effective measures concerning the chances and the social problems this new communication mode is bringing out or will bring out in the (near) future.

This chapter introduces a user perspective on VWs. It synthesizes research and arguments from communication science and media psychology to inform the multidisciplinary debate on VWs. Two questions will be discussed: What is so appealing about VWs? And which kind of effects should be expected from frequent use of VWs that are of primary relevance especially in legal and criminological contexts? Reflections on these key questions will allow to derive interdisciplinary research perspectives on today's and tomorrow's VWs. They shall also help to conclude specifications of demand for new thinking in terms of legal regulation and prevention of social problems that may become evident once VWs have become an integral part in modern societies' everyday life. Therefore, the chapter addresses the issues of motivational appeal of VWs (II.) and effects perspectives (III.). Consequently, three conceptual 'hotspots' for crossdisciplinary research on user issues in VWs are recommended as approaches to resolve the unique challenges that come along with the mass use of VWs (IV.).

2 The Motivational Appeal of Virtual Worlds

An analysis of why VWs are so attractive for users is indicated not only because it follows the growing importance of VW use as a common activity in need of scientific description and explanation. In the present context, this analysis is required to understand the motivational and social forces that underlie the growing importance of VWs and many of the concerns that law experts, criminologists, and many others holds in respect to VWs. For instance, issues of excessive or addictive use of VWs are closely connected to the fascination people experience during VW use (see teWildt this volume). Understanding what attracts people to VWs will thus be useful to derive perspectives on the regulatory and administrative challenges attached to VWs.

2.1 The Diversity of VWs

Explanations of people's interest in and sustained use of VWs conflict with the fact that contemporary VWs are highly diverse. In terms of technology, the most advanced type of VWs today are Massively Multiplayer Online Role Playing Games (MMOs), among which "World of Warcraft"® is the most prominent example. In MMOs, players typically control one individualized character and navigate through a large, complex virtual environment. Interacting with the (avatars of) thousands of other players and collecting digital objects of diverse kinds, users resolve tasks ("Quests") and organize in groups to meet major challenges. Modern "Game VWs" such as MMOs come along with highly impressive audiovisual representations and significant narrative complexity. With the opportunity to interact, communicate, and co-play with many other users, the bandwidth of appeal factors in MMOs is extraordinary (Yee 2006).

Other types of contemporary VWs are not so much centered around a virtual–fictional world, but rather rely on user-generated content and the co-creation of digital objects by users. "Second Life"® is the most popular and well-known example of this kind of VWs. Such environments allow users to customize a virtual representative (an avatar similar to most MMOs, see above) to occupy virtual space, build houses and visit places of other users. Rich interaction and communication opportunities allow for multiple applications, such as virtual work meetings, lectures in virtual classrooms, or all-virtual theater play.

Another important type of VW is social network sites such as "Facebook"®. While these platforms are less visual than MMOs and "Second Life"® in the sense that they do not provide a virtual–spatial environment that users can navigate through, they host virtual representations of many real individuals including images and textual self-descriptions. Links between user profiles make social relationships visible, and many modalities of user-communication are available that create substantial social dynamics and appeal (e.g., online groups of shared interest, message boards on individual profile-sites, and built-in channels of mediated interpersonal communication).

For each of these (and conceivable further) manifestations of VWs, specific literature on user motivations and everyday practice has been published (e.g., Yee 2006; Boyd and Ellison 2007). This chapter does not go into the details for all types of VWs, but rather distills general principles of user attraction that (should) apply to all kinds of VWs. This abstract approach is indicated to connect to requirements for law making and regulatory concepts that cannot be customized to any possible subtype of VWs, but need to focus on the core elements behind (virtually) all these subtypes in order to be efficient and effective.

2.2 *What Is in VWs for Users? General Principles of VW Appeal*

What do people find in VWs that creates their positive feelings during use and makes them return so frequently? What are the common characteristics of heterogeneous VWs such as "World of Warcraft"®, "Second Life"®, and "Facebook"®? Four fundamental principles of VW are proposed that address user motivations and desires in specific ways and can thus explain the motivational appeal of VWs.

2.2.1 Interactivity

A key characteristic of all VWs is interactivity (Rafaeli 1988; Vorderer 2000; Klimmt and Vorderer 2007). Unlike conventional mass media such as television, VWs invite and require users to take action themselves. Users launch events and actions that can be seen by themselves and by others, which creates a direct and personal relationship between the VW context and users' self. For video games, the experience of players' own efficacy ("effectance") has been found important to an enjoyable experience (Klimmt et al. 2007), and observing the effects of one's actions is clearly a universal motivation factor in all VW use. For instance, users who have construed a nice and complex building in "Second Life"® and receive positive feedback from other users stopping by certainly see 'what they have done' and associate positive feelings with it. The issue of publicity – there are always many others in VWs who observe, comment, interact – further adds to the importance of interactivity, for results of one's own activities are mostly not private and hidden, but presented to an arena of other people, some of which are typically relevant to the individual user (e.g., friends).

The broad appeal of VWs can thus partly be explained by interactivity that allows for active participation, construction, creativity, and, most importantly, the feeling of effectance and contribution. Instead of residing in the role of the witness or observer (as in TV use), users of VWs perceive themselves as co-designers of events displayed within the environment, which is highly motivating in different contexts (e.g., achieving a victory in an MMO, building a new relationship in "Facebook"®).

2.2.2 Interpersonal Communication

One element that distinguishes VWs from other interactive media, such as single-player video games or interactive television (Vorderer et al. 2001), is the Co-Presence of other users and the availability of communication channels that allow for interpersonal conversation. Early VWs relied on text messaging similar to chat communication (e.g., Curtis 1996), whereas modern technologies also facilitate voice communication so that different channels can be selected or combined. Nonverbal modes of interaction, such as exchanging items or simulating social behaviors through avatars, further add to the possibilities to communicate with other users. For Game VWs, interpersonal communication has been found a key explanation of their motivational appeal (Pena and Hancock 2006; Williams et al. 2007). VWs allow for easy access to vast numbers of individuals, and the interpersonal communication tools are used for most diverse social purposes, including organized game play, finding new friends, maintaining personal relationships over geographic distance, or even finding romantic partners (McKenna and Bargh 1999; Konijn et al. 2008; Steinkuehler 2006; Steinkuehler and Williams 2006; Walther 1996).

Because interpersonal communication is a key element of all VWs, it is also proposed as a general principle of VW attractiveness. It is especially attractive due to the fact that computer-mediated communication follows other social rules and conventions than face-to-face communication (e.g., Tanis and Postmes 2003), and one important of these differences is that individual communicators keep more control about their involvement with the communication situation. Users can withdraw from online conversations they find uncomfortable without having to fear negative consequences of violating conversation rules, for instance. Especially shy people seem to value the 'safer' mode of interpersonal communication in online VWs (Stritzke et al. 2004). Another major difference to face-to-face communication that renders conversations within VW attractive is easy accessibility of many different communication partners. Search tools (e.g., to find friends in "World of Warcraft" via avatar names) and public information about other users (e.g., individual profiles in social network sides with images and text descriptions) increase the accessibility of known and unknown communication partners and help to safe efforts that would be required in comparable situations of face-to-face communication (e.g., finding a friend in a crowded soccer stadium; finding out about the aesthetic preferences of a person one has just met). There are, of course, also less attractive dimensions involved in the interpersonal communication facilitated by VWs; most of them relate to the increased anonymity and the uncertainty about the trustworthiness of communication partners (e.g., McKenna and Bargh 1999; Walther 1996). Nevertheless, the diversity of opportunities and the specific circumstance of interacting with others is clearly an attribute of VWs that causes and sustains user interest and participation (Jansz and Tanis 2007; Klimmt et al. 2009).

2.2.3 Simulated Action Generates True Experience

VWs allow users to participate in a dynamic illusion of social or geographic space that hosts their own and other people's actions. For instance, in "World of Warcraft"®, players can choose from a variety of activities such as slaying monsters, collecting items, exploring new realms, or networking with other players (e.g., Chan and Vorderer 2006). Activities are simulated by the technology of the VW, for instance, mouse clicks are represented as a sword attack or a buying transaction by the "World of Warcraft"® software. In social network sites, activities include communication (such as posting comments on other people's profiles) and relationship building (such as making contact with people who share one's interest in a specific domain, cf. McKenna and Bargh 1999). Such social activities have, of course, real-life consequences (e.g., a user having a new friends after visiting a social network site), but during usage, VWs display, visualize and/or simulate user activities within its context frame. User activities can be complete illusions, that is virtual and fictional (such as the fight against a virtual monster in "World of

Warcraft"®), or mixed forms with a virtualized element such as visiting another user's virtual place in "Second Life"® and a real-life element such as agreeing on the date for a real-life meeting during that "Second Life"® visit. VWs thus serve as platform for users' isolated and/or social activities, and they create comprehensive representations of these activities, for instance displays of fighting game characters or of messages posted to another "Facebook" user's profile.

While these representations of what users are doing or have done are bound to the computer screen and are mostly virtual and immaterial in nature, they nevertheless allow for authentic, highly personal *experience*. For instance, players of MMOs may be well aware of the illusion inherent to their defeat of a horrible monster, yet they generate an experience of fear, suspense, heroism, and victory that is based on virtual action, but is real in terms of self-perception and emotion. Identification theory (Klimmt et al. 2009) argues for shifts in users' self-perception through virtual action: Users feel more courageous, powerful, important, and successful if they control their fighter avatar in an MMO than they would feel in an everyday life context (Bessiere et al. 2007). Similarly, the act of provoking a good friend by posting a mean message to his profile in a social network site is highly virtual (compared to a face-to-face provocation), yet it holds authenticity as (a) the friend is likely to notice the provocation, and (b) others can observe the provocation as well, so a virtual public sphere is being established. Thus, the provoker has good reason to be amused about a 'real' provocation, albeit it has been executed under highly virtualized circumstances. Consequently, VWs capability to host user actions of diverse kinds (including simulated actions in fantasy worlds and virtualized social activities) is argued as a general principle that binds user interest and sustains user participation. Because the virtualized user actions connect to real-life experience, the motivational benefits of performing activities in VW can claim affective and social relevance to users far beyond the stage of exposure to the VW itself (e.g., Klimmt and Hartmann 2008).

2.2.4 High Availability

A fourth issue in VWs' motivational appeal is that the highly diverse functionalities – fun, enjoyment, creativity, interpersonal relationships, and so on – are available at low cost, any time and, to the extent that mobile devices are used, also anywhere. Because VWs allow to pursue very different goals within one technological application (see above), they offer ways to satisfy diverse needs by clicking just one button. In the offline era, much *more* effort was required to pursue *fewer* goals, such as writing a letter to a friend in a foreign country, playing a single-player computer game and using a phone in another room to call a sibling. VWs frame diverse communication and leisure (sometimes also business) activities in one context that can be accessed with low effort. The high availability of this multi-purpose tool renders it highly attractive at least to those generations that have grown up or are growing up with computers (the so-called "digital natives", cf. Prensky 2001).

In sum, all types of VWs share some fundamental principles that attract many people and motivate frequent and repeated use, both in gaming or entertainment contexts and in social, creative or even work-related contexts. The authentic simulation of events and activities, and even more so the interpersonal conversation with other users render VW exposure and the events that happen within them personally relevant and socially dynamic. The high availability of VWs as integrated multi-channel leisure and communication platform suggests that VW use is an economic and rational decision in many situations of everyday life. With next generation VWs building on what is possible today, these fundamental principles of motivational appeal are likely to become even more salient in the future.

3 A Typology of Effects of Virtual Environments

Because VWs can help to pursue diverse goals of diverse people or the same people in diverse situations, there is a growing community that habitually attends to VWs or even relies on VWs as tool for accomplishing everyday life. With VWs becoming platforms of social gathering and rich interpersonal exchange, the breadth (number of people affected) and depth (intensity of impact) of the consequences of VWs for society are likely to increase. In this section, four dimensions of VWs are discussed that mark the importance of VWs for criminology and law studies. distinguishing the types of law-relevant impact is a fundamental task that needs to be resolved before empirical research and legal analysis can specify the problems and challenges that VWs impose on today's and tomorrow's justice system. The types of effects that will be discussed here are excessive consumption, interpersonal crime within virtual interaction contexts, new copyright issues, and stimulation of offline crime through exposure to VWs. Before this agenda for VW and crime research is laid out, some basic considerations that affect all types of VW effects are presented.

3.1 Preliminary Considerations

Because VWs are bound to technological innovation and facilitate frequent interpersonal communication, they attract particularly young people. In Germany, 97% of adolescents aged 12–19 use the Internet at least 'sometimes' (MPFS 2008), and about 33% of male adolescents use Multiplayer Online Games (MMOs, one important type of contemporary VWs) at least "several times a week" (MPFS 2008). Specific implications for crime research and prevention are bound to the developmental stage of adolescence, including the evolution and permanent negotiation of gender identity (e.g., Egan and Perry 2001). Some male adolescents are attracted to hypermasculine ("macho") attitudes and behaviors during their search for a masculine identity, and VWs are an important platform for learning and experimenting with masculinity issues (Jansz 2005). Another relevant implication of adolescence is a lack of experience with public communication and the potential consequences of one's own social actions. Publishing embarrassing party photos in an VW that was meant as personal provocation of a single individual may have severe, long-term, wide-range social consequences that many young users who publish such images seem not to be aware of. Finally, sensation seeking and curiosity are important drivers of behavior in adolescence (e.g., Greene et al. 2000), which increase the probability of young users being ready to try out unusual und potentially risky behavioral options in VWs, such as purchasing virtual goods or accessing extreme communication content (e.g., pornography, cf. Peter and Valkenburg 2006). While such behavioral patterns typical for adolescents must not be confused with a general lack of 'rationality' or 'literacy' in adolescent VW users, the prevalence of these patterns is a driver for criminological and legal concern, for (a) providers of VW may exploit these patterns for commercial purposes in problematic ways and (b) VWs may serve as powerful multipliers of effects of such behavioral patterns. For instance, VWs can amplify of social impact of mobbing and bullying, because they establish a public arena that is much larger and long lasting than the local context of schoolyard mobbing and bullying (cf. Li 2005). With more advanced VWs allowing to perform an increasingly diverse set of social activities (including conflict-related behaviors), this amplification capacity of VWs is likely to generate more criminological problems at the levels of individuals (e.g., new modes of victimization and guilt phenomena) and of society at large (e.g., commercial VW providers as controllers or moderators of interpersonal conflict behavior for large numbers of users).

A final fundamental issue that should be considered in the context of VW impact dimensions is the element of co-creation that is inherent to VWs. Because users interact with a platform provided by an organization or company and many other users to generate events, actions, and messages within the VW, various parties are involved in the social reality that happens in VWs. These parties are in many cases highly anonymous: Users can represent themselves with nicknames and fake identities, and most contributions from the platform provider are automatic, pre-programmed activities (such as monsters attacking in online video games). So the increasing social relevance of VWs is accompanied by the fact that much social activity is anonymized. This mixture is undesirable from a crime-related perspective, because anonymity motivates more extreme forms of antisocial behavior in many contexts (e.g., in car traffic situations, cf. Ellison-Potter et al. 2001) and because *accountability* and *responsibility* for events and actions occurring within VWs is often hard to determine. For instance, who is to be held responsible for cyber-stalking conducted within a social network site? A technically well-trained perpetrator may benefit from the anonymity of computer-mediated communication and hide his or her true identity while attacking a victim through repeated online communication. For providers of large social network platforms, it is virtually impossible to trace or to prevent individual antisocial communication, because the messaging functionalities of such VWs are fully automatic and operate without human moderators of user interaction.

3.2 Excessive Use

Since the ways VWs can be utilized are increasing rapidly, ever-new reasons for logging in frequently and to stay within a VW appear on a regular basis. Much social life can be organized and enjoyed through participation in VW, and other motives or goals, such as shopping, work meetings, or educational activities are becoming more and more common as well (see Keser this volume). Especially permanent game worlds such as MMOs and browser games have been criticized for their capacity to keep users playing for much longer amounts of time than they actually 'would want to play' and/or than 'would be good for them' (e.g., Lemmens et al. 2009; Peters and Malesky 2008; teWildt this volume). While there is still a great lack of research and reliable evidence on the causes, dimensions, and consequences of excessive or addictive VW use (e.g., Wood 2008), there is reason for concern from a regulatory perspective for two reasons. One is that providers of VWs could exploit the problems of individual users to regulate their participation in VWs commercially. Business models that rest on monthly user fees (e.g., many MMOs or "Second Life"®) are in structural conflict with the societal goal to prevent addictive behaviors and help those individuals suffering from such problems. So regulation issues emerge concerning the way VW providers monitor the usage patterns of their (often quite young) visitors and deal with potential risks of excessive use. The other reason why excessive consumption of VWs is problematic from a regulatory perspective is that for those highly problematic cases reported in the psychiatry literature (see teWildt this volume; Thalemann et al. 2007), the subjective dependence on a VW such as "World of Warcraft"® comes along with detrimental effects for work or school performance, family relationships, and individual well-being. These life consequences are in turn relevant to crime prevention, because they increase risks of transitions into criminal activities known from substance-based addicts ("drug-related crimes"). So far, there is no indication of a widespread 'addiction' epidemy in VW users, whereas there is evidence for positive effects for many users (e.g., satisfaction with social relationships, cf. McKenna and Bargh 1999). From a criminological perspective, however, addiction-related risks should be elaborated and monitored due to the expectable increase of importance of VWs in the future. The preliminary considerations introduced earlier apply to this issue: Young people, the key audience of most VWs, are particularly susceptible to excessive activity levels (such as addictions), and because individual users are handled fully automatically by the VW systems, there is a risk of diffusion of responsibility, as it is arguably difficult for platform providers to identify excessive users among millions of registered clients.

3.3 Interpersonal Crime Within VWs

With the increasing diversity of actions that VWs allow users to perform, the number of possible 'virtual' behaviors that are ethically or legally problematic is of course also growing. Early multi-user dungeons, for instance, were merely text-based interaction spaces that followed simple rules and only allowed a strictly limited set of user activities. Legal problems would only emerge from verbal insults that users could exchange, but there was not the same quality of public attention involved that is typical for contemporary VWs such as social network sites or MMOs. In contrast, state-of-the-art VWs have empowered users to choose from a vast number of behavioral options and thus have also expanded the list of possible wrongdoings. Using the messaging systems of VWs for antisocial communication, which is typically labeled as "flaming" (Douglas 2008) or "cyberbullying" (Li 2005), is probably the most common type of problematic behaviors found in VWs, which is also manifest in a significant number of thematic court hearings. Therefore, this type of 'virtual crime' has already received attention in criminology and law studies (e.g., Myers 2006).

However, the close resemblance of real life that is typical for today's (and certainly for tomorrow's) VWs opens the perspective on other modes of crime that is bound to VW contexts, including property crimes and quasiphysical offences. For instance, digital items become increasingly popular in many VWs. They are used as tools in game play, virtual accessories for online self-presentation, or other purposes such as paid work. Some of these digital items (e.g., a rare magic sword in an MMO) hold value for their owner because s/he invested much time and effort to acquire them, others hold rather objective value because they were purchased from a vendor for nonvirtual money (e.g., the operator of a VW), and some digital items hold psychological value because they are subjectively relevant to their owner, for instance, an avatar that reflects a user personality in a unique way due to its special look and dress. Manipulating, damaging, destroying, stealing, kidnapping, or hiding such digital items against the will of their owner are thus behaviors relevant to criminology and law studies (see Forgo, this volume; Laue, this volume). Because digital items are somewhat stable (as long as the VW operator secures their 'existence') and can hold different types of value, there is a huge potential of conflict in VWs concerning property crime and virtual damage to property delinquency. Technically, such behaviors only affect some bits and bytes on a remote server of the VW platform provider. However, in spite of their immaterial quality, such crimes *feel like real* property crime or damage to property from the view of the victim property owner (see sect. 2.2), so there is subjective suffering or loss of real-life investments (time, money) involved. It is therefore difficult to specify the legal status of such crimes, and things are even more complicated because corporate agents (the platform providers) are also involved with author rights in many respects: For instance, if a virtual sword is stolen in an MMO context, the MMO operator has 'created' the digital item and merely provided access to it to the owner. The whole existence of the sword is thus dependent on the VW company, which can theoretically make the sword (and thus the object of the virtual theft crime) vanish with a single mouse click. From this perspective, how much ownership can the victim of the theft crime actually claim, even if s/he had paid real-life money for it? The confluence of virtuality and reality in modern VWs thus generates both interesting and highly difficult challenges for criminology and law practice.

An even more severe form of VW-related interpersonal crime reaches beyond the harm that users can do to objects and avatars existing within a VW, the so-called "identity theft" (Whitson and Haggerty 2008). Perpetrators can conquer access to a user's controls over his digital self-representations and personal data, which allow for a variety of highly problematic crimes. For instance, identity theft enables illegal transfer of money from a victim's online banking account, the execution of problematic social behaviors 'in the name' of the victim (e.g., consumption of online pornography with the victim's user name) or the infliction of reputation damage by making the victim's avatar behave antisocially in the VW. Identity theft thus relates to a variety of real-world problems and damages, and is again a challenging confluence of virtuality and offline dimensions in terms of crime analysis, definition, judgment, and prevention.

One interesting implication of VW for interpersonal crimes is that most harmful actions can be executed by typing and mouse-clicking. Data manipulations or information theft is thus much less of a physical crime that the perpetrator can experience through her/his senses (as, for instance, real-life physical violence is). The virtuality of crime execution is interesting, because it suggests a lowered perception of severity and suggests a playful frame to interpersonal crime – in fact, much cyberbullying such as publishing embarrassing party pictures of distal victims in VWs may have begun as a playful joke, and perpetrators may have had 'nothing evil in mind'. The easiness of performing antisocial activity in VRs is important both for the explanation and for the prevention of VW crimes, and it also raises questions about guilt and perceptions of guilt in virtualized social environments.

3.4 New Copyright Issues

The protection of copyrights in the era of digital media has emerged as a major challenge for the justice system, because there are diverse instances of 'piracy' and similar copyright violations, and because the economic importance of those industries suffering from violations of their copyrights due to digital media is tremendous (Kranenburg and Hogenbirk 2005). VWs introduce new facets to this complex of legal issues. In general, copyright issues are complicated in VWs, because any events, utterances, and objects that appear within VWs and maybe object to copyright protection are generated with contributions of a (commercial) platform operator (such as "Linden Labs"®, the company that is running the metaversum "Second Life"®; see sect. 3.1).

To the extent that contemporary and future VWs allow users to create content individually and/or together with other users, there is a need to regulate copyright issues that emerge from these creative user contributions. For instance, in digital environments, it is easy to create digital copies of visuals, shapes, textures, brand names and other information that is copyright-protected in other Internet contexts and/or real life. Because such multiplication or reconstruction of existing protected material is easy, copyright violations are likely to appear frequently in large-scale VWs. Each single violation does not represent a case of severe damage to the copyright holder, of course; for example, a single avatar in "Second Life" that is wearing a user-created T-shirt with a copyrighted brand name on it will not affect the copyright holder's commercial and social interests significantly. However, if such violations of copyrights would occur in user generated content in huge numbers, a severe regulatory problem would result, because it is virtually impossible to trace, prosecute, and negotiate millions of bagatelle crimes.

Concerning user generated content in VWs that is not contaminated with copyright problems due to relationships with original materials under protection, other questions of copyrighting emerge. For instance, in co-creation of digital buildings, pieces of art, or messages, many users of a VW may be involved, and the platform operator is always participating by virtue of his or her digital infrastructure that is utilized. Who will own the copyrights of such co-created digital content that cannot exist without support from the VW operator and has been assembled by many individuals together? Who is responsible for negotiating such issues? In the case of global co-creation with contributors from five different continents: Which country should host court hearings in cases of conflict? In turn, if there is no conflict but consensus of shared copyright – is this copyright heritable if a rights-holder dies or is it portable if the platform operator is acquired by another company? VWs thus drive the problems concerning copyrights further because of the increasing amount of user-generated content and the mass diffusion of responsibility for copyright protection: Each user is 'a little bit' responsible, but it is difficult to exercise supervision and control of all the copyrighting behaviors within a VW.

Interestingly, the possibility to collaborate and interact with other users to actually create new objects within the virtual environment is one factor of motivational appeal in many VWs (e.g., Yee 2006; Sects. 2.1 and 2.2). Future VWs will continue to encourage mass production of user generated content for economic reasons, so the open questions concerning copyrights in VWs deserve attention from criminology and law studies to prevent escalation problems in the future.

3.5 Stimulation of Offline Crime Through Exposure to VWs

A final dimension of criminology-related implications of VWs is the outreach of VWs to the real world. While experiences during VW exposure (including virtual interpersonal crime, cf. Sect. 3.3) reach out to real-life contexts frequently (e.g., the disruptive effects of being cyberbullied, cf. Hinduja and Patchin 2008), VWs can have a stimulating or facilitating impact on the generation of criminal behavior that is performed completely outside of the VW and in real-life circumstances. The main issue that has been debated in this context so far is the impact of video game violence on real-life aggression (Anderson 2004; Hermann this volume; Hartmann this volume; Mathiak this volume). The rationale behind this research perspective is that frequent exposure to violent action in video games shapes users' motivational and cognitive configurations in ways that render the execution of antisocial behavior in real-life settings (e.g., interpersonal conflict) more likely (Bushman and Anderson 2002). Given the popularity of violent video games, this specific issue of VW impact on behaviors relevant to criminology is certainly justified. However, the list of real-world crime that may be stimulated or otherwise nurtured by VW use is much more diverse.

One perspective on VW impact on real-life crime is at the level of interpersonal relationships. As much communication and relationship building is going on among VW users (see Sect. 2.2), there are many phenomena of combined online and offline interpersonal contact among users, including preparation of dates in social network sites or 'clan meetings' of organized MMO players (e.g., Parks and Roberts 1998). From an interpersonal crime perspective, VWs can thus facilitate initial contact between perpetrators (e.g., burglars, impostors, stalkers) and victims. Communication and bonding within VWs may also allow perpetrators to collect information required for real-life crime execution (e.g., victim's address, daily routines, thematic interests). Due to the playful frame of communication among VW users (Klimmt and Hartmann 2008), there is also a risk of misinterpretation of online messages that result in problematic offline encounters (e.g., user jokes about sexual preferences communicated within a VW may be taken seriously by another users and lead to a confrontation in an offline context). At the level of interindividual crime, then, VW may serve as networking platform that bring perpetrator and victim together, or as tool for perpetrators to collect information about (potential) victims.

Another important perspective on VW's stimulation of real-world crime is at the level of groups and organizations. Extremist parties and terrorist networks use the Internet and VWs for various purposes, including internal messaging, propaganda, and recruiting of new members. They have been found to adopt the technical capabilities of online communication rapidly and effectively (Qin et al. 2007). For organizations who seek for large-scale real-world crime (e.g., terrorist attacks or intergroup violence), VWs can serve as communication tools that help to prepare real-world activity in various ways: They provide a public forum for advertising extremist positions and to attract media attention; they allow to execute organizational goals in virtualized yet globally accessible modes (e.g., islamist terror networks could symbolically attack Western buildings or avatars in VWs), and they allow to recruit individuals who are willing to execute offline crime in the name of the organization. All these virtual activities have stimulating consequences for organized real-world crime (Tsfati and Weimann 2002). From the perspective of the individual VW user, these organized activities enlarge the probability of contact with extremist positions and information, which is not by definition undesirable from the perspective of crime prevention. Nevertheless, with the adoption of VW-based communication modes by extremist organizations, new challenges arise for research and prevention in offline crime.

4 Conclusions: Hotspots for Future Research

While a communication science perspective on new media technology is often primed by public concern about negative effects, but inclined to achieve a balanced view of both chances and risks, the criminological perspective is necessarily focused on risks and socially undesirable implications. The analysis so far has found that virtual worlds and metaverses open new pathways for crime, both within and outside of their virtual context. With growing audiences and richer interaction possibilities, the profile of VW-related criminality is likely to become more diverse and relevant in the future. The fact that primarily young people are heavy users of VWs gives reasons for particular concern, for example, because adolescents are more likely to try out unusual (and unsafe) communication or transaction opportunities and are on average more susceptible to excessive activities and political propaganda. While one must not forget the profound positive consequence of VWs and metaverses for individuals and society at large (e.g., McKenna and Bargh 1999), there is a need for more systematic research and reflection on the criminological risks that come along with today's and future VW applications. In this section, three major themes are suggested as research objectives of primary concern. Making progress in research on these topics should allow to find effective responses to the challenges outlined so far, for they will allow for better explanation, prediction, and prevention of VW-related crimes. These proposed hotspots are the sense of right and wrong, media literacy, and the legal status of virtual locations, objects, and persons.

The Sense of Right and Wrong in VW Users Moral reasoning is an important factor in individual's decisions about criminal behavior (Bandura 2002). The anticipation and moral evaluation of consequences of behavioral options are keys to moral reasoning. Most people are likely to avoid the behavioral option of "punching" during an interpersonal conflict, for instance, because their moral evaluation of the damage that would follow from a punch is highly negative. The particularities of VWs, the communication among their users, and the crimes that can be performed within or with support from VW contexts suggest that users of VW do not apply the same moral standards, anticipations, and/or evaluations to what is happening in virtual contexts and in real-life contexts. Because of the playful and symbolic frame of social interaction in VWs (Klimmt and Hartmann 2008), perceptions of crime severity and negative consequences of interpersonal insult seem to be different for VW contexts. Moreover, the 'easiness' of illegal, harmful, and/or ethical problematic behavior in virtual contexts – everything can be done from the home computer with a few mouse clicks, whereas most offline crimes require much more effort and thus also more moral disengagement (Bandura 2002), is likely to alter users' view on what is truly problematic in virtual worlds compared to the normative standards in real-life contexts.

To study users' perceptions of right and wrong as well as possible differences in moral standards for individual conduct in VWs versus offline society would be informative to the criminological assessment of VWs in several ways. First, the motivational analysis, theoretical modeling, and empirical prediction of VW-related crimes would be greatly enhanced if the moral reasoning of VW users is better understood. Second, law making (e.g., definition of punishment levels for cyber-crime) and court decision making would benefit from more knowledge on how users (tend to) view moral standards in VW contexts. This does not imply to adopt (potentially lowered) moral rules for legal decision making, of course, yet it is important to consider perpetrator (and victim) morality in evaluating given cases of VW-related crime. Survey studies and field experiments conducted within VWs may be most promising research designs to learn more about the moral standards VW users apply and potential differences in these standards to what is common in offline contexts.

Media Literacy A second research hotspot is users' knowledge and abilities to participate in VWs effectively. Much criminological problems that emerge from the mass use of VWs may originate from perpetrators' lack of knowledge or wrong expectations about the consequences of their activities. Adolescent cyberbullies, for instance, may simply be unaware of VW and general Internet characteristics that amplify the impact of individual interpersonal crime in online environments, such as quick news diffusion to other web sources and long-lasting information storage that prevent erasing of an insult once it has been posted (Hinduja and Patchin 2008). What has been meant as a limited provocation or one-time expression of dislike may turn into a massive public attack with much more severe consequences than the originators had in mind. Media literacy, broadly defined in the present context as the general understanding of how VWs and online communication work, is thus likely to show up as an important moderator of many VW-related crimes: Those users who are highly VW-literate and thus aware of the potential consequences of their virtual behaviors should be less likely to engage in VW-related criminal activities than those users who lack such knowledge, because their moral reasoning in decision making will not include correct expectations about the consequences of their behaviors toward other users of objects in a VW.

Media literacy is also relevant to VW-criminology from a victim's perspective. Much VW-related crime is enabled or at least promoted by victim's lack of self-protection. For instance, many online users (particularly VW users) seem to be ignorant of the negative consequences of revealing personal, even intimate, data in online contexts. Especially young users of social network sites and other VWs have been criticized because of their generous sharing of personal data. Improved knowledge of how to communicate effectively and safely in virtual contexts may turn out as important contribution to reduce VW-related crime because this way, the number of opportunities for perpetrators would go down. This refers not only to the prevention of interpersonal (virtual) crime (Sect. 3.3), but also to users' susceptibility to organized criminal activity such as extremist organizations' presence in VWs for persuasion and recruiting purposes (see Sect. 3.5).

Legal status of virtual locations, objects, and personae. Finally, criminology should face the fact that VWs are going to evolve rapidly and conquer still more importance in modern societies of the future. From a communication perspective, which is focused on meaning and symbols, the events, actions, and relationships that exist in VWs are 'real', because they hold relevance to the involved users. Most legal and criminological reasoning is, however, still bound to the traditional, material world, and it is difficult to adopt conventional legal definitions (e.g., theft) to fully virtual events such as one VW user taking a digital item that belongs to another user. Thus, much VW crime is 'unreal' and difficult to handle from a criminology perspective (see Cornelius, this volume). Because so many people assign meaning and relevance to what they do and experience in VWs, law studies and criminology will need a new framework for legislation and court decision making that allows to handle the new types of crimes, perpetrators, and victims in a comprehensive and transparent manner. This new framework will have to define the legal status of the virtual, that is, to reproduce the digitalization and virtualization of social action that VWs have initiated. Virtual locations, digital items, and social representations of users will need more and effective regulation in the future, and new types of societal interests need to be protected.

The final concluding remark addresses research organization. Conducting successful research into the focal points of criminological interest proposed above – the sense of right and wrong, media literacy, and legal status of the virtual – implies to build effective interdisciplinary collaborations. Communication science is capable to provide a theoretical account of VW as a medium, and also methods for empirical user assessment. Social psychology has to offer frameworks for interpersonal relationships and conflict, and has studied the impact of computer-mediation in these contexts extensively (e.g., McKenna and Bargh 1999). Other disciplines, including philosophy and economics, should also contribute to advancing research on VWs and criminality. As virtual worlds will evolve as a ubiquitous, permanent 'second mode' of social interaction that can be activated anywhere and anytime and reaches out into almost all domains of social life, the challenge of crime analysis, prevention and prosecution will need transdisciplinary efforts to be resolved. The earlier such collaborative projects begin, the better will the justice systems be prepared for the virtual worlds of the future.

References

Anderson CA (2004) An update on the effects of playing violent video games. J Adolesc 27(1):113–122

Bandura A (2002) Selective moral disengagement in the exercise of moral agency. J Moral Educ 31(2):101–119

Bessiere K, Seay AF, Kiesler S (2007) The ideal elf: identity exploration in World of Warcraft. Cyberpsychol Behav 10(4):530–535

Boyd DM, Ellison NB (2007) Social network sites: definition, history, and scholarship. J Comput Mediat Commun 13(1):article 11. http://jcmc.indiana.edu/vol13/issue1/boyd.ellison.html, accessed on June 17, 2011

Bushman BJ, Anderson CA (2002) Violent video games and hostile expectations: a test of the general aggression model. Pers Soc Psychol Bull 28(12):1679–1686

Chan E, Vorderer P (2006) Massively multiplayer online games. In: Vorderer P, Bryant J (eds) Playing video games: motives, responses, and consequences. Lawrence Erlbaum, Mahwah, pp 77–90

Curtis P (1996) Mudding: social phenomena in text-based virtual realities. In: Kiesler S (ed) Culture of the internet. Lawrence Erlbaum, Mahwah, pp 121–142
Douglas KM (2008) Antisocial communication on electronic mail and the internet. In: Konijn E, Utz S, Tanis M, Barnes S (eds) Mediated interpersonal communication. Routledge, New York, pp 200–214
Egan S, Perry D (2001) Gender identity: a multidimensional analysis with implications for psychosocial adjustment. Dev Psychol 37(4):451–463
Ellison-Potter P, Bell P, Deffenbacher J (2001) The effects of trait driving anger, anonymitiy, and aggressive stimuli on aggressive driving behavior. J Appl Soc Psychol 31(2):431–443
Greene K, Krcmar M, Walters LH, Rubin DL, Hale JL (2000) Targeting adolescent risk-taking behaviors: the contributions of egocentrism and sensation-seeking. J Adolesc 23(4):439–461
Hinduja S, Patchin JW (2008) Cyberbullying: an exploratory analysis of factors related to offending and victimization. Deviant Behav 29(2):129–156
Jansz J (2005) The emotional appeal of violent video games for adolescent males. Commun Theory 15(3):219–241
Jansz J, Tanis M (2007) Appeal of playing online first person shooter games. Cyberpsychol Behav 10(1):133–136
Klimmt C, Hartmann T (2008) Mediated interpersonal communication in multiplayer video games: implications for entertainment and relationship management. In: Konijn E, Tanis M, Utz S, Barnes S (eds) Mediated interpersonal communication. Routledge, New York, pp 309–330
Klimmt C, Vorderer P (2007) Interactive media. In: Arnett JJ (ed) Encyclopedia of children, adolescents, and the media. Sage, London, pp 417–419
Klimmt C, Hartmann T, Frey A (2007) Effectance and control as determinants of video game enjoyment. Cyberpsychol Behav 10(6):845–847
Klimmt C, Schmid H, Orthmann J (2009) Exploring the enjoyment of playing browser games. Cyberpsychol Behav 12(2):231–234
Klimmt C, Hefner D, Vorderer P (2009) The video game experience as 'true' identification: A theory of enjoyable alterations of players' self-perception. Communication Theory 19(4): 351–373.
Konijn E, Tanis M, Utz S, Barnes S (eds) (2008) Mediated interpersonal communication. Routledge, New York
Kranenburg H, Hogenbirk A (2005) Multimedia, entertainment, and business software copyright piracy: a cross-national study. J Media Econ 18(2):109–129
Lemmens JS, Valkenburg PM, Peter J (2009) Development and validation of a game addiction scale for adolescents. Media Psychol 12(1):77–95
Li Q (2005) New bottle but old wine: a research of cyberbullying in schools. Comput Hum Behav 23(4):1777–1791
McKenna KYA, Bargh JA (1999) Causes and consequences of social interaction on the internet: a conceptual framework. Media Psychol 1:249–269
MPFS (2008) Jugend, information, Multimedia 2008 [Adolescence, Information, Multimedia 2008]. MPFS, Stuttgart
Myers DA (2006) Defamation and the quiescent anarchy of the internet: a case study of cyber-targeting. Penn State Law Rev 110(3):667–686
Parks MR, Roberts LD (1998) 'Making Moosic': the development of personal relationships on line and a comparison to their off-line counterparts. J Soc Pers Relationships 15(4):517–537
Pena J, Hancock JT (2006) An analysis of socioemotional and task communication in online multiplayer video games. Commun Res 33(1):92–109
Peter J, Valkenburg P (2006) Adolescents' exposure to sexually explicit material on the internet. Commun Res 33(2):178–204
Peters CS, Malesky LA (2008) Problematic usage among highly-engaged players of Massively Multiplayer Online Role Playing Games. Cyberpsychol Behav 11(4):481–484
Prensky M (2001) Digital natives, digital immigrants. On Horiz 9(5):1–6

Qin J, Zhou Y, Reid E, Lai G, Chen H (2007) Analyzing terror campaigns on the internet: technical sophistication, content richness, and Web interactivity. Int J Hum Comput Stud 65(1):71–84

Rafaeli S (1988) Interactivity. from new media to communication. In: Hawkins RP, Wiemann JM, Pingree S (eds) Advancing communication science. Merging mass and interpersonal communication processes. Sage, Newbury Park, pp 110–134

Steinkuehler C (2006) Massively multiplayer online video gaming as participation in a discourse. Mind Cult Activ 13(1):38–52

Steinkuehler C, Williams D (2006) Where everybody knows your (screen) name: online games as 'third places'. J Comput Mediat Commun 11(4):article 1. http://jcmc.indiana.edu/vol11/issue4/steinkuehler.html

Stritzke WGK, Nguyen A, Durkin K (2004) Shyness and computer-mediated communication: a self-presentational theory perspective. Media Psychol 6:1–22

Tanis M, Postmes T (2003) Social cues and impression formation in CMC. J Commun 53: 676–693

Thalemann R, Wölfling K, Grüsser S (2007) Specific cue reactivity on computer game-related cues in excessive gamers. Behav Neurosci 121(3):614–618

Tsfati Y, Weimann G (2002) www.terrorism.com: terror on the internet. Stud Confl Terrorism 25(2):317–332

Vorderer P (2000) Interactive entertainment and beyond. In: Zillmann D, Vorderer P (eds) Media entertainment: the psychology of its appeal. Lawrence Erlbaum, Mahwah, pp 21–36

Vorderer P, Knobloch S, Schramm H (2001) Does entertainment suffer from interactivity? The impact of watching an interactive TV movie on viewers' experience of entertainment. Media Psychol 3(4):343–363

Walther JB (1996) Computer-mediated communication: impersonal, interpersonal, and hyperpersonal interaction. Commun Res 23:3–43

Whitson K, Haggerty KD (2008) Identity theft and the care of the virtual self. Econ Soc 37(4): 572–594

Williams D, Caplan S, Xiong L (2007) Can you hear me now? The impact of voice in an online gaming community. Hum Commun Res 33:427–449

Wood RT (2008) Problems with the concept of video game "addiction": some case study examples. Int J Ment Health Addict 6:169–178

Yee N (2006) Motivations for play in online games. Cyberpsychol Behav 9(6):772–774

Crime Potential of Metaverses

Christian Laue

Abstract With the development and spread of metaverses open to the public, criminology could face a new challenge. From the point of view of criminology, metaverses can be looked at from three different perspectives: First, there is the question whether metaverses open new dimensions to the already known Internet criminality. Looking at this more thoroughly, there is the danger of a quantitative increase of criminality in the Internet, but only low potential for the development of completely new forms of criminality. Second, virtual worlds can be regarded as separate societies for which the effects of deviant behaviour can be analysed by criminology, this resulting in severe conceptual and methodical problems. The findings of criminology in the real world can hardly be applied to the conditions of the virtual world. Finally, the use of virtual worlds could have feedback effects on the users in their real life. By imparting certain values and attitudes, the (excessive) occupation with virtual worlds could have effects on the behaviour in the real society. This question can so far hardly be answered and should be the object of further research.

1 Introduction

A Metaverse – a term usually attributed to Neal Stephenson's novel "Snow Crash" – denotes a social virtual world. In this lecture, I will be looking at the "crime potential of Metaverses" in three different ways. The first question to ask is: To what extent do Metaverses open new dimensions of cyber crime? Do new opportunities for criminal activity result from Metaverses, whether quantitatively or even qualitatively? In this context, Metaverses must be considered and categorised as part of cyber crime. They

C. Laue (✉)
Institute of Criminology, University of Heidelberg, Heidelberg, Germany
e-mail: laue@krimi.uni-heidelberg.de

K. Cornelius and D. Hermann (eds.), *Virtual Worlds and Criminality*,
DOI 10.1007/978-3-642-20823-2_2,

are thus regarded as part of existing cyber crime or as part of cyber crime that still needs to be developed.

Second, Metaverses can be seen as individual little societies in which deviating behaviour can lead to certain effects, which are comparable to the disturbances and irritations caused by criminality in real society. The question is whether deviating behaviour – which has to be defined as criminal – can lead to similar effects in Metaverses as crime does in real society. The consideration of social virtual worlds may even allow conclusions to be drawn about the causes and effects of crime in real society. Thus, Metaverses could be regarded as laboratories of real criminology: an attractive idea for every criminologist. In the following, I would like to call this the "criminology of Metaverses".

While, in the first part of the lecture, Metaverses are viewed from the outside as separable parts of the Internet and, in the second part, from the inside as individual societies, it would only be logical to conclude by highlighting the links between the virtual and the real worlds. The issue that concerns us here is the knock-on effects that virtual worlds have on the real lives of users and how these can influence their behaviour in the real world. It is likely that virtual worlds convey certain attitudes and skills to their users as well as shortcomings that influence their real behaviour.

2 From the Outside: Metaverses as a New Challenge for Cyber Crime

Criminology, especially German criminology, has thus far paid little attention to cyber crime. When you look through the major German general literature on penal law, it is striking that the keyword "cyber crime" often does not feature at all (see Göppinger 2008). Only short papers can be found, such as the one by Eisenberg, who treats cyber crime as a manifestation of economic crime. For him, cyber crimes or multimedia crimes are "those criminally relevant acts that are committed using data networks (especially the Internet)" (Eisenberg 2005, Sect. 47 marginal no. 69).

There are hardly any other publications on cyber crime. This is astonishing since every year the Police Crime Statistics report highlights the rise in Internet-related crime. The Ministers of the Interior of the German federal states are convinced that the Internet offers great potential for crime [see, e.g., the Federal German Minister of the Interior, Wolfgang Schäuble (2007), during the opening of the BKA-Conference (German Federal Bureau of Investigations) "Tatort Internet" in 2007].

The "Polizeiliche Kriminalstatistik (PKS)" (German Police Crime Statistics) – usually taken as an initial guide to gain an overview of the extent and development of the overall number of crimes or types of offenses – has reported a separate category, "computer crime", since 1987. This category comprises a number of criminal acts for which the use of a computer is required or is at least helpful to carry them out. The term "computer crime" is based on criminal law and does not report cyber crime as a separate category.

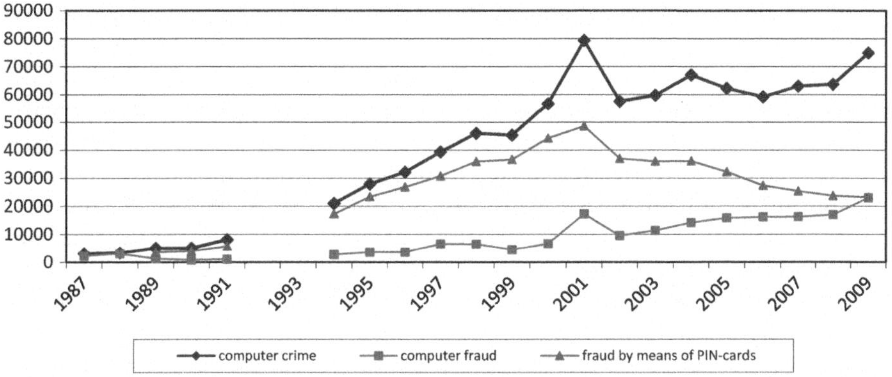

Fig. 1 Computer Crimes from 1987 to 2009. Source: BKA (German Federal Bureau of Investigation, edt.): Polizeiliche Kriminalstatistik 1987–2009

For our purposes, however, the PKS is of minor importance only, since the collective term "computer crime" includes hardly any cyber crimes, but rather fraud offences (such as computer fraud according to Sect. 263a StGB (German Criminal Code) or fraud by means of PIN cards obtained illegally).

Nevertheless, the PKS at least provides a rough overview of the development of cyber crime. In 2009, 74,911 computer offences were recorded in Germany, which is 1.2% of the total number of offences (6,054,330). In the first 15 years in which computer crimes have been recorded separately, the absolute figures of offences recorded have increased 26 times to almost 80,000 in 2001. Although the German reunification has to be taken into consideration, the rise is nevertheless constant, which is hardly surprising as, during these years, the computer has become indispensable in globalised society. It is much more amazing that there has been no further rise in computer crime from 2001 onwards, but rather stagnation. This is very remarkable, especially in the context described here, since the Internet has become extremely widespread during this period. In Europe, the number of Internet users has risen from 106 million at the end of 2000 to 385 million in 2008 (according to Internet World Stats 2009) (Fig. 1).

2.1 Types of Cyber Crime

Following David Wall (Wall 2001), four types of cyber crime in particular are identified internationally:

(a) "Cyber trespass": Trespassing on and/or damaging another person's computer, e.g. by "hacking" or sending viruses.
(b) "Cyber thefts/deception": Theft of material and also immaterial resources through piracy as well as credit card fraud via the Internet. Now famous is

the so-called "scam" or advance fee fraud, where the scammers pretend to transfer vast sums of money from Third World Countries– first by ordinary mail, later – in extended version – by e-mail. This kind of fraud promises the receipt of a huge commission after acceptance of a large sum of money; the victim has, however, been persuaded to make advance payments. Since this kind of fraud originated in Nigeria in particular, and Nigeria has reacted by implementing its own penal law (Sect. 419 of the Nigerian Penal Code), it is also called the "419 scam". This type of crime has increased significantly through the use of the Internet.

Another kind of Internet fraud – in a non-technical sense of the term – is "phishing". Faked e-mails prompt the victim to reveal sensitive data, especially bank details, which the offenders can use to gain access to the victim's fortune.

(c) "Cyber pornography/obscenity": The Internet provides various new ways of transmitting and selling pornography. It is estimated that 2–12% of all websites have pornographic content. Child pornography is especially problematic as the Internet is excellently suited to the cheap production, circulation and transmission of pornographic images of children. The market for child pornography has been significantly expanded by the Internet and is difficult to control. It may be assumed that the Internet has considerably promoted the worldwide sexual abuse of children, since the market for its distribution has become much bigger.

(d) "Cyber violence": This term comprises all forms of psychic damage or incitement to physical damage – known as Internet stalking and cyber bullying.

There is one form of cyber crime that can be subsumed under cyber aggression and to which special attention is given in Germany: content-related Internet crime. Especially due to the punishability of the "Auschwitzlüge" (Auschwitz Lie) according to Sect. 130 of the German Criminal Code – an element of a crime that only exists in a handful of countries – statements/comments are punishable in Germany which, in other countries, are covered by the freedom of opinion. This shows that cyber crime can really have regional references.

2.2 *New Dimensions of Cyber Crime by Metaverses?*

The situation outlined above raises the question: What new opportunities for criminal activity do Metaverses provide?

(a) Cyber trespass

The danger of cyber trespass is probably not increased any more through the participation in virtual worlds than it is through the general use of the Internet.

(b) Cyber theft/deception

There are probably various new opportunities for cyber theft and cyber deception in social virtual worlds like Second Life, where business is conducted using currencies that can be changed into real money. According to Sect. 263 StGB, it is a punishable fraud if someone knowingly sells a virtual object that in fact does not correspond to the requirements agreed upon or assumed upon purchase. The Internet is an enormous temptation for dishonest traders, since the impression of anonymity and non-apprehendability is given by the ability to hide behind user names or avatars. In fact, the access requirements to the Internet in many cases allow people to log in with an invented identity.

The potential theft of virtual objects is much more difficult to judge from a legal point of view and is also a new kind of offence, which is only conceivable in a social virtual world. The aim of Second Life is that users buy objects, such as shoes, to adorn their avatar and create a unique external appearance. These objects must be paid for with Linden Dollars and are thus property of the buyer. Where there is property, there are also potential thieves. If one avatar takes the objects bought by another avatar, this is, however, not fraud in the sense of Sect. 242 StGB, since this element of an offence presupposes the removal of a movable object, i.e. a physical object. The shoes bought in Second Life are, however, not physical objects, but rather virtual objects, i.e. immaterial pixels. They can only be "taken away" by programme manipulations. Such behaviour would be criminally relevant as computer fraud/deception according to Sect. 263a StGB, assuming an unauthorised action on a computer programme – this would be the criminal relevance in the real world. In the virtual world, however, it would be theft, since one avatar takes away a thing from another avatar. We have to bear in mind that such an act – the virtual "theft" – is only possible in a virtual world in which the users can own property. In this respect, it is possible that Metaverses bring about new forms of criminal behaviour.

Cyber currencies in virtual worlds are only a quantitatively new dimension, although, supposedly, a very large one. Metaverses offering economic activity with a currency of its own that can be exchanged into real money are an invitation for money laundering. It is, however, questionable whether the economic system in Second Life will really be a central point of contact for money launderers. The Internet is already an ideal place for laundering illegal money (see Rederer 2000). Cyber currency, numerous business opportunities and an almost free choice of location already offer everything to disguise money laundering and to make it almost uncontrollable. Second Life could play a certain role in the circuits required for this because it offers all the ingredients for money laundering. However, it is not sufficient to be just an entrepreneur in Second Life to legalise illegal money without control. The large amount of publicity Second Life has experienced should lead to closer monitoring of any attempts to launder money there. Second Life could be another field of activity, but only one among many offered by the Internet. Metaverses are not generally expected to lead to a qualitatively new dimension of money laundering.

(c) Cyber pornography/obscenity

Social Metaverses offer new ways of distributing pornographic images. In 2007, Second Life ran into problems because individual users had designed avatars that looked like children and these were presented in pornographic images, which is punishable according to Sect. 184b StGB. There is no restriction of punishability due to the fact that these images are only fictitious for, according to general opinion, the term child-pornographic publications according to Sect. 184b StGB includes fictitious images, too (Kusch 2000). The virtual child pornographic images with avatars as subjects and objects were presented extensively – especially in Germany – in the media and Second Life came under great deal of pressure.

It was also easy to buy real, i.e. non-fictitious child pornographic images by e-mail from Second Life users and to pay for these with Linden Dollars. Some of the members use the opportunities for business activity provided by Linden Lab to disseminate child pornographic images. This can be seen at least as a quantitative extension of the possibilities of the Internet.

The distribution of pornographic publications to minors, which is punishable according to Sect. 184 StGB, is also problematic. Second Life does not have any effective age controls, which means that minors can easily log in. It is thus relatively easy for them to consume the pornographic images offered by Second Life. However, the virtual worlds do not extend the possibilities already offered by the Internet on websites such as "www.youporn.com", which have no effective age controls either.

To sum up, it can be said that social virtual worlds in particular present new ways of distributing pornography, especially with regard to the fictitious presentation of child pornography. This is, however, not a qualitatively new distribution channel. Instead, Second Life, for example, offers an additional distribution channel via the Internet. Indeed, Second Life is not primarily a pornographic site; the main focus is still on other content. Sexuality and pornography are just part of a very large spectrum of possible content in virtual worlds. There is, however, a danger that pornographic distribution possibilities are concealed within the Second Life world where, on the one hand, potentially many users can be reached and where, on the other hand, the investigation authorities have very little control. The operators of virtual worlds should make it their mission to reduce such misuse. Very often, the police's hands are tied in this respect (Report Mainz (ARD) broadcast of 7 May 2007).

(d) Cyber violence

For some people, the Internet has become an important social space. It not only provides information, knowledge and entertainment, but also the possibility to make social contacts. It is reported that the social contacts of some people are even reduced exclusively to the Internet. It is therefore not surprising that this development also leads to aggression and social violence.

The fate of the 13-year-old Megan Meier, who committed suicide in October 2006 after having been abandoned by her assumed, but fictitious Internet love, became well-known all over the world. This fictitious Internet character called "Josh Evans" had been created by a former schoolmate and her mother and neighbour of the victim's family in the Internet chat room "MySpace", and succeeded in charming Megan completely. In order to humiliate her, Josh one day finished the relationship with nasty insults and exposed her on the Internet. Megan was unable to cope with this and hung herself that afternoon. In November 2008, the then 49-year-old mother of the schoolmate was sentenced for computer fraud by an American Federal Court because she had logged herself in at "MySpace" with a false name. Meanwhile, Missouri has passed new legislation concerning cyber bullying, which sets an example for other legal systems.

The fact that this case did not happen in a Metaverse, but in the well-known and widespread "MySpace" shows that this kind of bullying is not reduced to virtual worlds, but was already possible in the existing Internet. It is precisely in this respect, however, that a social virtual world such as Second Life opens up many possibilities. The "ingredients" for such bullying all exist in Second Life: the establishment of social contacts among virtual characters is the declared aim of Second Life. It seems clear that the exploitation of the difference in authority – as in the case of Megan Meier: a grown-up offender and a minor victim – is obvious and even encouraged. But this is a general danger of the Internet and its possibilities to make, but also to abuse social contacts.

It is worth mentioning two similar cases from Germany here: On March 30, 2009, the so-called "Chat room Murderer" Christian G. was sentenced to life imprisonment. He had met women via the Internet and then met up with them in the real world, causing the death of two of these women. At first glance, it seems doubtful that these offences are really caused by the Internet. However, when you read that the accused had virtually no social contacts in real life and that he was only able to make contacts by creating a second – virtual – existence, the opportunity to make social contacts via the Internet is perhaps not a sufficient condition for the offence, but is a necessary one.

This becomes clearer when you consider the famous case of the "cannibal of Rotenburg", Armin Meiwes. In February 2001, he killed and ate a man he had met via the Internet and who had given his consent to being killed and mutilated. In this case, it is difficult to imagine that the offender and consenting victim would ever have met outside the Internet. Here too, the Internet seems to have been a necessary condition for the offence. There is some controversy as to whether it makes sense to count such a case as a cyber crime. It is characteristic in each case that the offenders would hardly have come into contact with their later victims without the help of the Internet. In the case of the "cannibal", the Internet offered the extremely low probability of meeting a consenting victim. The range of potential social contacts was significantly widened by the Internet. In the case of the "chat room murderer", he was able to construct a virtual identity, which deviated from his real identity, and thus make himself much more attractive to real contacts.

Metaverses also offer the opportunity to construct virtual identities – this is even their objective to a large extent. However, Metaverses are not a new dimension of the Internet for committing crimes since – as shown by the two cases above – these possibilities already exist on the Internet.

Social virtual worlds, however, pose another challenge for a criminological discussion. On the one hand, there is the criminologically relevant behaviour of the users in the virtual world, and on the other hand, possible repercussions between the use of a virtual world and behaviour in the real world.

3 Metaverses from the Inside: Criminological Research

Some virtual worlds, especially Second Life, regard themselves as a separate society offering their users an individual social field of activity that should be as similar as possible to real society. Users can make social contacts, they can invest, found enterprises, have economic success, they can be creative or – more passively – enjoy their spare time and travel or just use artistic or entertainment programmes.

In such an environment, there is always the possibility that individuals show deviant behaviour and thus damage other individual avatars/users or the virtual community as a whole. This socially damaging behaviour could be described as criminal.

Social virtual worlds are seemingly opening up unforeseen possibilities for criminological research: Would it not be possible to conduct criminological research e.g. in Second Life – a relatively manageable area compared to the real world – and then draw conclusions on criminological relationships in the real world? Second Life as a kind of a social laboratory, which – on human rights grounds – would not be possible in the real world; a field of experiments just to answer criminological questions?

If Second Life is an image of real society in virtual space, the same mechanisms and social laws must surely apply as in real life. Criminologists could then conduct their research in a manageable framework and, e.g., empirically verify the well-known theories on the origins of crime in the laboratory situation of virtual space. This is a tempting idea. A closer look at this, however, reveals three counter-arguments.

3.1 The Problem of Measuring Crime in Metaverses

It is probably very difficult to measure the number of crimes in virtual worlds. In the real world, crime statistics give us a rough idea of the extent and development of crimes – despite all the reservations against them. These statistics form an indispensable basis for numerous research projects and they do not exist in the virtual world. It would, of course, be possible to interview the users, and this would correspond to the interviews of so-called "dark field" research. These would have to be modified – the intensity of the use of the virtual world would, e.g., have to be measured since Second Life users are only part-time users, whereas citizens of the real world are always citizens. Details on offenders or victims would have to be put into relation to the extent and use of the virtual world. This obstacle, however, could be overcome.

3.2 The Problem of Crime Definition in Metaverses

What does crime in the virtual world really mean? This question is much more difficult to answer. The question of how to define a crime adequately is a problem not satisfactorily solved in criminology and is one that might perhaps never be solved. There is a formal notion of "crime" in criminology: crime is a behaviour defined as criminal by the legal system. Judging crime in the virtual world is compounded by even more problems, since such a formal evaluation is impossible. Second Life itself deliberately avoids regulating the behaviour of its avatars. Thus, the only option would be to recourse to the national or international legal systems of the real world. This would inevitably result in different assessments/evaluations, since e.g. the "Auschwitz Lie" of Sect. 130d StGB – a very important offence concerning the German legal assessment of the Internet – would hardly have a counterpart in other countries and would thus be of no relevance for other researchers. The international comparability of possible results would be very limited.

There would only be a small number of offences that could be examined sensibly. As already mentioned, a theft in the virtual world – by far the most frequently committed offence in the real world – would be computer fraud in the real world. Finally, most of the deviant behaviour which, in the real world, is an element of a crime of the core criminal law – theft, robbery, damage to property, arson, rape, bodily injury or homicide – can only be reduced to a computer offence: computer fraud, modification of data, or computer sabotage.

3.3 The Problem of Crime Effects in Metaverses

Finally, we must take a look at the persons in question, or rather the avatars. It is questionable whether deviant behaviour in virtual worlds can really lead to such social damage as in the real world. The possibilities of victimisation are already significantly reduced: a homicide or murder offence is hardly conceivable in Metaverses, since it is a characteristic of a virtual world that every participant has a number of or even an unlimited number of lives. If an avatar loses its life – and this happens very often in many online games – it cannot really be regarded as the victim; this is at least not remotely comparable to victimisation in the real world. Thus, potential crimes in virtual worlds lose much of their threatening effect.

There could be effects in the area of fraud or virtual theft. The economic activity promoted by Second Life could really be brought to a standstill if acts of fraud were carried out on a massive scale, because honest entrepreneurs would lose interest. An effective control would be necessary here, and it could be interesting for criminological research to observe how order could be brought to a world with a self-selected lack of rules.

This, however, only touches on a small portion of crime; the types of crimes that are particularly important to the real general public hardly play a role in virtual worlds.

You also encounter problems when you consider the offenders. When an avatar is insulted, who is the offender? Who must be punished – in as far as it is hoped that punishment will have any effect at all? And, if the avatar is punished – there might be the possibility of sending him to a virtual prison – who would actually be affected by the punishment? Ultimately, the user behind the avatar is responsible and only he can feel the punishment. This means there is no punishment for the behaviour of the avatar but only for the behaviour of the person sitting in front of the computer.

Thus, the view of the virtual world as an autonomous society is, in most cases, inadequate. Only in cases where real social acts are directly transferred to the virtual world – especially with regard to commerce in Second Life – can real social findings be transferred to the virtual world.

4 Repercussions of Metaverses on Reality

The third interesting problem for criminology concerns how the use of virtual worlds affects the behaviour of users in the real world.

I will only touch on this briefly here, since the following lectures will go into more detail. Concerning the question of the effects of Internet use, a possible increase in the willingness to use violence – after numerous relevant cases – is at the focal point of criminology and also criminal policy. A number of violent acts at American and European schools seem to have been inspired by computer games; it is, however, doubtful whether these are to be attributed to Metaverses. This will certainly become clearer in the following lectures.

Less obvious is the possibility that Metaverses which, in many cases, are a monopolising social counter-world, are able to create and care for values and attitudes among their users. There are reports about people spending more time in virtual worlds and on the Internet than in real society whose social contacts are concentrated on the Internet, in short, people who spend more time with avatars than with human beings. These replacement worlds could tend to create their own values and norms. If these values and norms are contrary to the values and norms of real society, subcultures emerge. And if these socials worlds have an influence on their users, it may be possible that they will take the values and norms of the virtual world and apply them to the real world. This and the resulting conflict between the norms and values of virtual society and those of real society could influence the behaviour of the users and, probably, also increase crime. So far, little research has been conducted in this field, although it could prove to be worthwhile.

5 Summary

In summary: The existence of Metaverses does not call for new criminology. A qualitatively new dimension of crime is possible only in marginal areas; in most cases, Metaverses simply provide new fields of investigation for the now well-known cyber crimes. There remains, however, inadequate research in this field in Germany.

References

Bundeskriminalamt (2009) Polizeiliche Kriminalstatistik Bundesrepublik Deutschland. Berichtsjahr 2008. Bundeskriminalamt Wiesbaden

Eisenberg U (2005) Kriminologie. Beck, München

Göppinger H (2008) Kriminologie. Beck, München

Internet World Stats (2009) http://www.internetworldstats.com/stats.htm. Accessed 30 Jun 2011

Kusch R (2000) Aus der Rechtsprechung des BGH zum Strafverfahrensrecht. Neue Zeitschrift für Strafrecht Rechtsprechungsreport:289–320

Rederer E (2000) Geldwäsche mit Cybermoney. Oder: Wie tradierte Bekämpfungsstrategien wertlos werden. Kriminalistik. Unabhängige Z kriminalistische Wissenschaft Prax 54:261–269

Report Mainz ARD (2007) "Second Life." Tummelplatz für Kinderpornografie, 7 May 2007. http://de.youtube.com/watch?v=Wk8uNWF77gg. Accessed 16 Mar 2010

Schäuble W (2007) Tatort Internet – eine globale Herausforderung für die Innere Sicherheit. Rede zu Beginn der BKA-Konferenz. http://www.bmi.bund.de/cln_165/SharedDocs/Reden/DE/2007/11/bm_bka_herbsttagung.html. Accessed 16 Mar 2010

Wall DS (2001) Cybercrimes and the Internet. In: Wall DS (ed) Crime and the Internet. Routledge, London

Is Virtual Violence a Morally Problematic Behavior?

Tilo Hartmann

Abstract This chapter pursues the question whether virtual violence is a morally problematic behavior. Virtual violence is defined as any user behavior intended to do harm to perceived social agents who apparently try to avoid the harm-doing. This chapter reviews existing literature that suggests that users hurt themselves if they get engaged in virtual violence (e.g., become more aggressive) and that users may also harm other users if they direct their violent acts against their avatars. Recent research is reviewed that further suggests that users may intuitively perceive virtual agents as social beings. They may thus intend to do harm to other social beings (instead of objects) when conducting virtual violence. The chapter also tackles (and denies) the idea that autonomous virtual agents are living entities that may suffer from virtual violence. In light of the reviewed evidence, virtual violence is considered a morally problematic behavior.

> Nobody feels guilty about kicking a rock for the simple pleasure of doing so, but doing the same thing to a child is universally forbidden. What's the difference? (Pizarro et al. 2006, p. 82)

Ethics deal with the question whether one should or should not engage in a certain behavior. In many cultures violence is considered an ethical issue. Many societies developed norms (and even laws) that tell about justified (or legal) violence and unjustified (or illegal) violence. Norms primarily seek to protect potential victims from harm-doing. However, developing norms about violence does not only protect potential victims, but also potential perpetrators. From a normative perspective that values a socially stable environment and the minimization of pain, violence may also harm perpetrators, because it may reinforce or intensify dysfunctional or even pathological personality characteristics (Anderson and Bushman 2002a; Berkowitz

T. Hartmann (✉)
Department of Communication Science, VU University Amsterdam, The Netherlands
e-mail: t.hartmann@fsw.vu.nl

K. Cornelius and D. Hermann (eds.), *Virtual Worlds and Criminality*,
DOI 10.1007/978-3-642-20823-2_3,

1993). Restricting violence does therefore not only help to protect potential victims, but also perpetrators.

Ethical and legal concerns about portrayals of violence in the media are widespread and have been pronounced for decades (Anderson and Bushman 2002b; Geen and Thomas 1986; Slater et al. 2003). Traditionally, concerns focused on detrimental effects of observing violence that is imitated by human-made technology (e.g., in television, music, books). Surprisingly, related discussions and (psychological) theories did not always draw a sharp distinction between the observation of real-world violence and violence in the media. An abundance of studies confirmed detrimental effects of observing violence in the media (e.g., Anderson and Bushman 2002b), but the specific implications of observing mediated violence remained somewhat unclear.

The growing popularity of new and interactive media, particularly video games and online virtual environments, revived – and intensified – existing concerns about media violence. In violent interactive environments, people may not only observe violence, but also act out violence themselves. Thus, dysfunctional effects on the user may be even greater than the ones observed for noninteractive media such as television (Paik and Comstock 1994). Indeed, an abundance of studies conducted within Psychology and Communication Sciences suggest that playing violent video games induces short-term aggression (Anderson 2004). In addition, a growing number of longitudinal studies suggest long-term aggressive effects on the user as well (Anderson et al. 2007; Anderson et al. 2008; Hopf et al. 2008; Möller and Krahé 2009; Slater et al. 2003). In light of these findings, an ethical debate about virtual violence seems to be justified. Accordingly, politicians and lawmakers of key video game countries such as the United States, UK, or Germany started to discuss whether access to violent video games needs to be restricted in order to protect users (i.e., perpetrators of virtual violence) from becoming more aggressive.

This chapter contributes to the discussion about ethical implications of virtual violence. Both, users' intention to do harm to others if they engage in virtual violence, and the actually inflicted harm may be considered important aspects when deriving an ethical judgment about virtual violence. This chapter therefore aims to illuminate whether users can be considered intentional aggressors, and whether users actually harm themselves and other users (and even other virtual agents) if they engage in virtual violence. The discussion will be primarily based on social–psychological approaches. The existing debate about violence in video games and other virtual environments has not been free of misunderstandings about the subject, however. Therefore, a clear definition of virtual violence seems to be a necessary first step.

1 Virtual Violence

Discussions of virtual violence, i.e., violent behavior in interactive media environments, should be based on a definition of the term. Past definitions of media violence exist, but they do not seem to reflect the specific characteristics of virtual violence.

1.1 Some Problems of Past Definitions of Media Violence

Violence (or physical aggression) in the real world is commonly defined as "any behavior following the intention to do harm to others who are motivated to avoid the harm-doing" (Baron and Richardson 1994, p. 7). The same definition is often used to define *media* violence: "Violent media are those that depict characters intentionally harming other characters who presumably wish to avoid being harmed" (Anderson et al. 2008, p. 1068). For two reasons, Anderson et al.'s definition may not sufficiently characterize *interactive* virtual violence, however.

First, the definition is about the media, and not about the user. It seems to consider users as *observers* of violence in the media, which is indeed typical for noninteractive media (e.g., television), and may also occur in interactive settings (e.g., video games). However, observation is not a significant characteristic of interactive settings. The significant feature of interactive settings is that users actively manipulate the environment, i.e., they are agents. In violent video games and in other violent interactive settings, users *are* aggressors, rather than merely observers. Users tend to adopt the role of the character they play (Bailenson and Yee 2005; Blascovich and McCall in press; Eastin and Griffiths 2006; Shapiro and McDonald 1992; Yee et al. 2009), instead of merely directing the character like a string-puppet. With more natural interfaces (input-systems and feedback-loops), users' adoption of the game character's role may only become stronger. Accordingly, it is a characteristic of virtual violence that it is the user that is intending to do harm (Huff et al. 2003), which should be reflected in a definition.

A second issue that deserves clarification when adapting the definition of Anderson et al. (2008) is linked with the phrase about "characters who presumably wish to avoid being harmed". From a strict objective perspective, a character that wishes to avoid being harmed has to be a biologically existing agent, and probably a quite intelligent one, as simple living life forms may not pursue intentional behavior. However, today's media (or human made technology) are not able to create agents that would match the requirements of biological existence (e.g., Dorin 2004). Accordingly, in a strict objective perspective, media is not capable to give birth to characters that can suffer from harm-doing, or who may wish to avoid being harmed.

Contemporary media technology can only create the *illusion* of living entities. Accordingly, media can only provide the illusion of harm-doing. Eventually, it is up to the user to believe in the illusion of violence (Blascovich and McCall in press). The user must believe that s/he is intending to do harm to a biologically existent agent. Anderson et al. (2008) reflect this notion by speaking of "characters who *presumably* wish avoid being harmed". Media provides only imitations of reality. Accordingly, media violence is eventually a perceptual phenomenon; media content is only violent in the eyes of a certain user. If users seriously doubt the illusion, however, they may only see pixels on a screen instead of characters, red-colored sprites instead of blood, or well-programmed software scripts, instead of violent actions. If users of violent video games, for example, perceive other things than scared characters and aggressive harm-doing when they move their cross-haired mouse cursor over animated dots of ink that resemble the shape of a human body, it may be misleading to label their action "violent".

1.2 Defining Virtual Violence

A definition of virtual violence should reflect two aspects, then. First, in interactive media settings, violence is not only observed, but users become aggressors as they adopt the role of their game characters. Second, virtual violence requires the perception of others that presumably can be harmed, but apparently try to avoid being harmed. Accordingly, virtual violence may be defined as *any user behavior intended to do harm to perceived social agents who apparently try to avoid the harm-doing.*

2 Ethical Implications of Virtual Violence

Real-world violence is restricted by law to protect potential victims from being harmed. Virtual violence, in contrast, has become a legal issue primarily because perpetrators, that is, (adolescent) users, may harm themselves (i.e., become aggressive). The discussion in this chapter will apply an easy but intuitive rationale to ponder the ethical implications of virtual violence. First, virtual violence only seems to be morally problematic if there is a victim, i.e., a *life form* or a social agent that is *harmed.* Second, focusing on the *outcome* of violent behavior, virtual violence may be considered the more problematic, the more severe the harm-doing (cf., outcome-based ethics/utilitarian ethics/"Verantwortungsethik", Weber 1919). Third, one may also focus on a morally wrong *intention* when judging behavior (cf., intention-based ethics/deontological ethics/virtue ethics/"Gesinnungsethik"; Weber 1919). Virtual violence may be considered problematic, because it involves the intention of a user to do harm to other social agents that presumably wish avoid being harmed.

Because the actual amount of inflicted harm is crucial when judging the ethical implications of virtual violence, it seems helpful to differentiate between the (human) user and (virtual) agents as potential victims. Based on such a differentiation, three questions arise. With respect to *users* as victims, one may ask to what extent a user can actually be harmed by virtual violence. Are users hurting themselves if they commit virtual violence as aggressors? (question 1)[1] Virtual violence can be directed not only against autonomous virtual characters, but also against avatars that belong to other human users. Are other users hurt if their avatars become victims of virtual violence? (question 2) One may also consider autonomous *virtual agents* as victims

[1]The intention-based approach to judge virtual violence will also be considered when tackling question 1. The underlying questions are whether users indeed intend to do harm to other social beings (as presumed in the definition of virtual violence) and whether they play violent video games or commit violent acts in other virtual environments.

of virtual violence. Such a notion seems far-fetched on a first glance, as harm can only be done to living entities. Today's virtual agents can hardly be considered living entities, however.[2] A third question arises that is therefore the most philosophical one: can a (future) media character be harmed? (question 3).

2.1 *Question 1: Are Users Victims of Virtual Violence?*

Virtual violence can be considered a morally relevant behavior if it has detrimental effects on the (human) user that engages in such behavior.

2.1.1 Users May Harm Themselves

In the past, an abundance of studies from different scientific disciplines such as Social Psychology, Neuropsychology, and Communication Sciences investigated the effects of playing violent video games on aggression (Anderson et al. 2007; Anderson 2004; Bushman and Anderson 2002). Reviews reveal that most studies focused on short-term effects on players. Related studies have shown that playing violent games temporarily increases a player's aggressive thinking, feeling, behavioral intentions, and even behavior (e.g., Anderson 2004). An increasing number of longitudinal studies also examined the effects of repeated violent game play on the personality of players (e.g., Anderson et al. 2007; Hopf et al. 2008; Möller and Krahé 2009; Slater et al. 2003). The existing longitudinal studies suggest that more aggressive people prefer violent video games more than less aggressive people, and that playing violent games reinforces and may even increase aggressive personality characteristics.

In light of the converging evidence that playing violent games increases aggression, it appears that users harm themselves if they engage in virtual violence. The likelihood to get harmed by virtual violence can be compared to other potentially harmful behaviors, such as the risk to get lung cancer from passive smoking at work (Bushman and Anderson 2001). But the problematic outcome of virtual violence (i.e., becoming aggressive) may be considered less dramatic than the one of passive smoking (i.e., getting cancer). Still, it seems reasonable to conclude that virtual violence is a morally problematic behavior, because it seems to affect users in a problematic and harmful way.

Two critical remarks may be made, however. First, problematic outcomes of virtual violence have been primarily examined in the past in the context of playful

---

[2]It needs to be noted, however, that the conditions that constitute life or a living agent are lively debated among philosophers, biologists, computer scientists, and engineers (e.g., Ray 1992). Readers that like to learn more about this debate may also consult the scientific journal "Artificial Life".

environments such as video games. Little is known so far if the observed aggressive effects apply to other virtual environments as well (McCall et al. 2009). Second, the present chapter defined virtual violence as harm-doing against *perceived social agents*. Past research has shown that users of violent video games may become aggressive. But most studies did not take users' subjective perceptions into account. Therefore, it is not totally clear whether the observed effects on aggression are indeed due to virtual violence as it is defined in the present chapter, i.e., users' intentional harm-doing against *perceived social* agents who apparently try to avoid the harm-doing.

In order to ethically judge not only violent video game play, but virtual violence, a closer look on how users' perceive other agents and violent situations depicted in virtual environments seems to be necessary. Exploring how users perceive virtual violence not only promises to illuminate problematic outcomes of virtual violence, but may be also particularly helpful in revealing potentially problematic intentions of users.

2.1.2 Users May Follow Problematic Intentions

Only a few studies exist to date that shed light on how users subjectively experience virtual violence. Neuropsychological research conducted by Mathiak and colleagues (see Mathiak this volume; Weber et al. 2006; Mathiak and Weber 2006) shows that users' brain activity during violent video game play resembles the brain activity one would expect in similar situations in the real world. In their study players suppressed their emotions if they engaged in violent actions in a video game, i.e., they tried to "cool down". Results further suggest that the activity of brain regions that are important for empathetic feelings toward others was diminished during acts of virtual violence. In sum, the findings of Mathiak and colleagues indicate that users respond in a quite natural way on violence depicted in virtual environments.

Hartmann and colleagues (Hartmann and Vorderer in press; Hartmann et al. under review) suggest that virtual characters are getting increasingly less artificial and may thus develop into "something" a user cannot easily discard as an object, but may rather intuitively consider "some sort" of social and moral entity (Dorin 2004; Elton 2009). Referring to the initial quotation by Pizarro et al. (2006), violence against today's agents that are populating virtual environments may have less in common with kicking a stone, but may be more appropriately understood as a form of interpersonal aggression against another social being. In accordance with social–psychological dual-process models (e.g., Epstein and Pacini 1999; Smith and DeCoster 2000), Hartmann et al. (under review) suggest to differentiate users' spontaneous (automatic) perceptions from their more reflective (elaborate) perceptions of violence. Upon conscious reflection, users are likely to be aware of the artificial nature of media violence. Therefore, they probably consider the depicted violence to be "just a game" or to "have nothing to do with the real world" (Klimmt et al. 2006; Ladas 2002).

However, users' *automatic perceptions* of violence may evoke another sensation. In two studies, Hartmann et al. (under review) explored guilt as an indicator of users' automatic perceptions while playing violent games. Guilt can be defined as "the dysphoric feeling associated with the recognition that one has violated a personally relevant moral or social standard" (Kugler and Jones 1992, p. 218). Guilt should indicate if players' recognize to violate a moral or social standard if they engage in violent video game play. If users would discard video game violence as completely artificial while playing (as many avid players claim upon conscious reflection), guilt would be an improbable response. Why should anybody feel guilty for "removing a sprite from a computer screen"? Players' would not feel to do something wrong if they were fully aware that they do not hurt somebody, but are actually only immersed in an illusion. In such a case, guilt is an unlikely response. In addition, guilt should also not vary between different levels of justification of the conducted violence, nor should it relate to other determinants known to affect guilt in the real world (e.g., violence against innocent children vs. violence against male soldiers). To the extent, however, players intuitively perceive their violent actions (and the victims) to be meaningful if not to say: real, they may feel guilty for what they do, especially if the conducted violence is considered unjust and if players are rather empathetic persons.

In the two studies conducted by Hartmann et al. (under review), justification of video game violence and users' trait empathy indeed determined guilt in a structurally similar way as in real-world scenarios: people felt guiltier if they engaged in unjust violence, especially if they were empathetic persons. Similar to the conclusion drawn by Mathiak and colleagues, the findings suggest that, to a certain degree, players fail to acknowledge the artificial nature of the depicted violence.

A plausible explanation of this result is that users' automatic processes precede their more reflective processes while using a virtual environment (Bargh 1994; Smith and DeCoster 2000). Automatic (i.e., intuitive, spontaneous, impulsive) responses are quickly triggered by the media environment, and can only be subsequently regulated upon conscious reflection (Zillmann 2006). Reality-fiction distinctions, which are key in the separation of the media world from the real world, apparently require operations of the reflective system (Smith and DeCoster 2000; Zillmann 2006). In contrast, the automatic system seems to be incapable to judge what is mediated and what is not; accordingly, everything that is automatically perceived is subjectively real. Automatic processes seem to quickly form the impression of an apparent reality, even if the sensory input was created by media or other human-made technology (Dorin 2004). The intuitive perception of virtual agents as social agents seems to accompany such an apparent reality, just like emotions that follow on automatic appraisals of the environment (Roseman 2001). Even moral judgments may be intuitively processed (Haidt 2001). Thus, feelings of guilt may have already been triggered before more conscious or reflective elaborations about the displayed media environment set in. Accordingly, automatic social perceptions, emotions, and moral judgments may all already exist, before users are even able to blend in their knowledge that "this is not real" or "this is just a medium".

Editing or regulating perceptions, emotions, and moral judgments once they occurred is, in psychology terms, quite effortful. It may be doubted if media users are able and actually want to fully regulate or discard their automatic experiences (e.g., Harris 2000). First, a constant flow of incoming sensory information fuels the automatically established apparent reality, which in turn constantly contradicts the more reflective notion that "this is not real" (Meehan et al. 2002). Second, in the heat of a video game play or while being engaged in other interactive environments, users may lack the cognitive resources to fully regulate their automatic impressions. Third, users may only rarely ever be motivated to continuously discard their sensation of an apparent reality. Moviegoers, book readers, video gamers, and users of other virtual environments all rather seem to enjoy believing in the automatically created illusion for a while (Harris 2000). Indeed, research on media entertainment suggests that the enjoyment of most media offerings is much higher if users are able to believe in their apparent reality (Green et al. 2004), whereas reminders of the artificial nature of the depicted environment can be quite annoying (e.g., a program error, a badly designed character, a totally implausible behavior).

Taken together, it seems plausible that users of virtual environments may indeed engage in virtual violence as defined in the present chapter, i.e., they may indeed have the (automatic) feeling to do harm to another social agent that seemingly tries to avoid the harm-doing (Mathiak and Weber 2006; McCall et al. 2009; Dorin 2004). To the extent users intentionally pursue their behavior, even though they believe they are harming a social agent instead of an object or "pixels on the screen", their intention seems to be morally problematic (Powers 2003). Intending to hit another virtual agent does not seem to be the same as the intention to hit, for example, a figure in a chess board game, then. The intention to hit a virtual agent resembles the precarious intention of real-life aggression much more than the harmless intention to hit a chess figure.

2.2 Question 2: Can Other Users Be Victims of Virtual Violence?

Many virtual environments feature mediated user-to-user interactions (cf., Konijn et al. 2008). A user directs his or her avatar to interact with another avatar that is navigated by another user. Both users may feel to communicate to each other if their avatars perform symbolic behavior. User-to-user interactions that are processed through the virtual cloaks of avatars can turn violent as well if users try to harm the avatar of another user that wishes to avoid being harmed (e.g., Hunter and Lastowka 2003). The most severe form of harm-doing against another user is referred to as "online player killing", in which a player eventually kills another user's character inside the game world (Whang and Chang 2004, p. 596). The question arises to what degree users may feel harmed if their avatar becomes a target of virtual violence and eventually dies in the virtual environment? Research that examined this question is growing. Most publications, however, entail theoretical discussions and only include anecdotal evidence of harm-doing, in place of systematic empirical examinations.

Suler and Phillips (1998) provide a detailed review about different deviant behaviors in virtual environments. Based on the anecdotic evidence, their report also describes hate and violence avatars that may make use of offensive language. Effects on potential victims are not examined, however. Powers (2003) provides a philosophical discussion of the question if "the harms that some people claim to have suffered in cyberspace [are] real moral wrongs?" (p. 192). Based on the speech act theory, he argues that virtual performances are a part of authentic social practices. As such, they are intentional, meaningful, and thus often powerful enough to hurt other users. "For these reasons, it makes sense to speak of moral patients as having suffered real moral wrongs, and accordingly to assign blame to moral agents for having committed these wrongs" (p. 192). However, according to Powers, virtual harm-doing may still not be morally problematic if it adheres to the (explicit or implicit) set of rules of virtual environments. Just like it is not considered unfair if a boxer hits his opponent in the face in an official box fight (e.g., Bredemeier and Shields 1986), virtual violence may be a fair action if does not violate the rules of the virtual environment.

Huff et al. (2003) discuss a virtual rape that occurred in the text-based multi-user environment LambdaMOO. They come to the conclusion that "perhaps the most important lesson is that virtual actions and interactions have consequences for flesh-and-blood persons and hence, the flesh controllers of virtual action, whether they control directly (as in playing a character) or indirectly (as in designing a virtual world), have responsibilities for their actions" (p. 19).

A virtual rape is an extreme example of virtual violence, but even more common events than virtual rapes may cause harm to other users. In a study about the very popular Massive Multiplayer Online Role-Playing Game (MMORPG) "Lineage", Whang and Chang (2004) note that a common event such as a virtual death can be "a traumatic experience for some players, since dying comes with severe penalties with various consequences such as losing valuable player items or damaging the abilities of players, causing time losses" (p. 596). However, similar to Powers (2003), they concede that there are also legitimate forms of online player killing if the action adheres to the official rules and norms of the environment. Whang and Chang assume that a "fair killing" of another avatar may also lead to less traumatic user experiences.

Wolfendale (2007) stresses that users' *attachment* to their avatars may strongly influence how much pain is caused it the avatar is hurt or even killed. Wolfendale's bases her approach on the view that "avatar attachment is expressive of identity and self-conception and should therefore be accorded the moral significance we give to real-life attachments that play a similar role" (p. 112). Many players feel attached to their characters. As people that seek enjoyment, they are also emotionally engaged in the online world. As a consequence, they may easily feel hurt if their character is harmed. Therefore, especially virtual violence against avatars of highly involved users may be morally problematic: "Attachment to people, possessions, ideals, and communities means that we suffer when these are harmed. If we accept such suffering as the normal human condition and as the price we pay for the joy that attachment can bring us, then there is no reason not to accord avatar attachment the same moral standing common experience for many participants who are emotionally engaged in the online world" (p. 118, see Dorin 2004, for a similar notion).

In sum, it appears that other users *can* be harmed if their avatar becomes a victim of virtual violence, although systematic empirical evidence is lacking. The reviewed anecdotal evidence suggests that users feel hurt if their avatar is harmed, the more they feel attached to their character, the more the harm-doing violated existing environment-based norms and related expectations, and the greater the loss of time and monetary resources that have been invested in the virtual character. Because it is wrong to hurt another user, it also seems to be wrong to hurt or even kill another avatar if the user of an avatar felt emotionally attached to the virtual character, if the harm-doing violated game- or environment-specific rules, and if the killing implies the loss of a reasonable investment of time and money. Accordingly, virtual violence that is directed against other users' avatars may be a morally problematic behavior because it may hurt other users as well.

2.3 Question 3: Can a Media Character Be Harmed?

Today's media characters can probably not be regarded living entities (e.g., Boden 2000; Dorin 2004; Floridi and Sanders 2004; Ray 1992). Therefore, they cannot be harmed. But it seems a worthwhile philosophical question if human-made technology, specifically computer technology, may be capable to generate life forms, i.e., living virtual creatures, one day (a related discussion may also shed some light on the life status of today's virtual characters). Eventually, today's media technology may only be considered an intermediate step on the way to more advance technologies. A brief look into the discussion about computer-generated artificial life therefore helps to clarify whether virtual creatures may qualify for potential victims of virtual violence one day.

Since the rise of computer systems, a lively debate evolved about the possibility of *artificial* life (so-called "Alife", e.g., Searle 1980) and particularly virtual artificial life ("Soft Alife"; e.g., Ray 1992).[3] Life has been characterized in many ways, but *self-organization*, including metabolism, emerged as a core criterion of life in many related discussions (Boden 2000). Skeptics such as Boden (2000) argue that virtual artificial life is impossible, because electronic systems (e.g., software programs or simulations) lack a physical body that would be able to metabolize in a strict biological way: "Metabolism [. . .] is the use of energy-budgeting for autonomous bodily construction and self-maintenance, and no actual body construction goes on in simulations of biochemistry" (Boden 2000, p.122). Other researchers, however, stress the evolutionary underpinnings of life and argue that software programs may

[3]It has to be noted that the main goal of research on artificial life is to *model* life in order to explore and understand it. The debate about *actually* living software systems (instead of software that merely imitates, simulates, or models life) is not of central importance to the general field.

evolve – and thus may indeed come to life – within a digital environment (Ray 1992; Spafford 1989). Computer viruses, for example, have been discussed (but also rejected) as a form of artificial virtual life, as they resemble a self-replicating organism (Spafford 1989). Similar discussions evolved around whether or not a virtual agent (e.g., software) may develop into a moral agent one day (e.g., Anderson and Anderson 2007; Floridi and Sanders 2004), and if software systems can develop consciousness (e.g., McDermott 2007) or are capable to think (Searle 1990).

A full review of these and related discussions goes certainly beyond the scope of this chapter. It appears, however, that skeptics that doubt the possibility of artificial virtual life (Soft ALife) outnumber the researchers who propose that virtual life may be possible. If the skeptics are right, ethical considerations of virtual violence do not need to consider any actual harm that is inflicted upon a virtual agent, simply, because virtual agents are not really alive: not today, but probably also not in the future.

3 Conclusion

This chapter aimed to contribute to the discussion about ethical implications of virtual violence. Related social–psychological literature (and literature from neighbored disciplines) was reviewed in order to illuminate virtual violence, and particularly the harm-doing that results from such behavior. The reviewed evidence suggests that users risk to hurt themselves if they enact the role of an aggressive character, because they likely become more aggressive (and thus support socially dysfunctional states and personality characteristics). From this perspective, virtual violence can be considered ethically problematic behavior.

The reviewed literature suggests that users may also harm other users if they hurt their avatars. The existing empirical evidence, however, is much scarcer compared to the abundance of studies that proved aggressive effects. The reviewed literature suggest that other users may only be harmed if they felt emotionally attached to their avatars and thus suffer if their avatars are hurt or even killed. The killing of an avatar may be especially distressful for users if it implies the loss of considerable time and money. The killing of an avatar, even if it induces distress in the other user, may be still a just behavior, however, if the violence adheres to the (official or unwritten) rules of the virtual environment (Bartle 2009). Such an argument would be analogous to the justification of violence in sports (e.g., boxing), which certainly also implies distress and a loss of invested time and money for those athletes that are hurt (Bredemeier 1985). Still, the violent action may be considered appropriate, as all athletes willingly entered the violent situation and thus were able to expect potential negative outcomes.[4] In the same manner, virtual violence may not be

[4]The given example may also be misleading, as it may not fully match the definition of violence that underlies the present chapter. An important part of the definition of violence is that the potential victim apparently tries to *avoid* the harm-doing. The opponents of a box-fight (or in any

automatically wrong, simply because other users are hurt. Virtual violence that hurts other users should be considered morally problematic behavior, however, if it clearly violates (official or unwritten) the rules of the virtual environment.

Virtual violence may not only be problematic, because it has detrimental effects on users (as agents) and sometimes also on other users. According to the reviewed literature, virtual violence may also be problematic, because it builds on the intention of a user to actually hurt another social agent. Intentions are meaningful. They tell something about the state of mind of agents. Intended behavior provides a message. If users intentionally engage in virtual violence, even though they intuitively perceive other virtual agents as social beings, their behavior would be problematic. Not because of negative effects, but because of an ill "wanting" of the users. Next to detrimental effects of virtual violence, it is probably the irritating symbolical significance of users' intentions to do harm to others that raises moral concerns about virtual violence (e.g., Dorin 2004).

To conclude: Is virtual violence a morally problematic behavior? It appears that virtual violence is an ethically relevant behavior. Virtual violence features problematic intentions and effects that are worth to be ethically considered and evaluated. In light of the literature that is reviewed in this chapter, one may conclude that virtual violence is indeed a morally problematic behavior.

References

Anderson CA (2004) An update on the effects of violent video games. J Adolesc 27:133–122

Anderson M, Anderson SL (2007) Machine ethics: creating an ethical intelligent agent. AI Mag 28(4):15–58

Anderson CA, Bushman BJ (2002a) Human aggression. Annu Rev Psychol 53:27–51

Anderson CA, Bushman BJ (2002b) The effects of media violence on society. Science 295:2377–2379

Anderson CA, Gentile DA, Buckley KE (2007) Violent video game effects on children and adolescents. Oxford University Press, New York

Anderson CA, Sakamoto A, Gentile DA et al (2008) Longitudinal effects of violent video games on aggression in Japan and the United States. Pediatrics 122:1067–1072

Bailenson J, Yee N (2005) Digital chameleons: automatic assimilation of nonverbal gestures in immersive virtual environments. Psychol Sci 16:814–819

other violent sports competition) may certainly appear to avoid being harmed. However, the fact that they willingly entered the violent situation beforehand contradicts the notion of a victim that tries to avoid being harmed. The same applies to users that willingly entered a violent virtual environment. Accordingly, it may not be fully correct to label behavior "violent" that aims to do harm to those who willingly entered the violent situation (and expected the possibility to be harmed). This is not to say that virtual violence would never be harmful under those conditions, because it can still "amount to destruction of property, albeit in an environment where that is an expected outcome of participation" (Dorin 2004, p. 108).

Bargh JA (1994) The four horsemen of automaticity: awareness, efficiency, intention, and control in social cognition. In: Wyer RS Jr, Srull TK (eds) Handbook of social cognition, 2nd edn. Erlbaum, Hillsdale, pp 1–40
Baron A, Richardson DR (1994) Human aggression, 2nd edn. Plenum, New York
Bartle R (2009) MMO morality. Invited keynote held at the Game Cultures Conference, March 19–21, Magdeburg
Berkowitz L (1993) Aggression. Its causes, consequences, and control. Temple University Press, Philadelphia
Blascovich J, McCall C (2010) Attitudes in virtual reality. In: Forgas JP, Cooper J, Crano WD (eds) The psychology of attitudes and attitude change. Psychology Press, New York, pp 283–297
Boden MA (2000) Autopoiesis and life. Cogn Sci Q 1:117–145
Bredemeier B (1985) Moral reasoning and the perceived legitimacy of intentionally injurious sport acts. J Sport Psychol 7:110–124
Bredemeier B, Shields D (1986) Athletic aggression: an issue of contextual morality. Sociol Sport J 3:15–28
Bushman BJ, Anderson CA (2001) Media violence and the American public. Scientific facts versus media misinformation. Am Psychol 56(6/7):477–489
Bushman BJ, Anderson CA (2002) Violent video games and hostile expectations: a test of the general aggression model. Pers Soc Psychol Bull 28(12):1679–1686
Dorin A (2004) Building artificial life for play. Artif Life 10(1):88–112
Eastin MS, Griffiths RP (2006) Beyond the shooter game: examining presence and hostile outcomes among male game players. Commun Res 33(6):448–466
Elton M (2009) Robots and rights: the ethical demands of artificial agents. http://www.abdn.ac.uk/philosophy/endsandmeans/vol1no2/elton.shtml, accessed on June 15, 2011
Epstein S, Pacini R (1999) Some basic issues regarding dual-process theories from the perspective of cognitive-experiential self-theory. In: Chaiken S, Trope Y (eds) Dual-process theories in social psychology. Guilford, New York, pp 462–482
Floridi L, Sanders JW (2004) On the morality of artificial agents. Mind Mach 14:349–379
Geen RG, Thomas SL (1986) The immediate effects of media violence on behavior. J Soc Issues 42:7–27
Green MC, Brock TC, Kaufman GF (2004) Understanding media enjoyment: the role of transportation into narrative worlds. Commun Theory 14:311–327
Haidt J (2001) The emotional dog and its rational tail: a social intuitionist approach to moral judgment. Psychol Rev 108:814–834
Harris PL (2000) The work of the imagination. Blackwell, Oxford
Hartmann T, Vorderer P (2010) It's okay to shoot a character. Moral disengagement in violent video games. Journal of Communication 60:94–119
Hartmann T, Toz E, Brandon M (2011) Just a game? Unjustified virtual violence produces guilt in empathetic players. Media Psychology 14(1):339–363
Hopf WH, Huber GL, Weiss RH (2008) Media violence, youth violence, and achievement in school – a two-year longitudinal study. J Media Psychol 20(3):79–96
Huff C, Miller K, Johnson DG (2003) Virtual harms and real responsibility: a rape in cyberspace. IEEE Technol Soc Mag 23(2):323–330
Hunter D, Lastowka FG (2003) To kill an avatar. Legal affairs. Retrieved online from http://www.legalaffairs.org/issues/July-August-2003/feature_hunter_julaug03.msp, accessed on June 15, 2011
Klimmt C, Schmid H, Nosper A, Hartmann T, Vorderer P (2006) How players manage moral concerns to make video game violence enjoyable. Commun Eur J Commun Res 31(3):309–328
Konijn E, Tanis M, Utz S, Linden A (2008) Mediated interpersonal communication. Lawrence Erlbaum, Mahwah
Kugler K, Jones WH (1992) On conceptualizing and assessing guilt. J Pers Soc Psychol 62(2):318–327
Ladas M (2002) Brutale Spiele(r)? Wirkung und Nutzung von Gewalt in Computerspielen [Brutal players? Use and effects of violent video games]. Peter Lang, Frankfurt

Mathiak K, Weber R (2006) Towards brain correlates of natural behavior: fMRI during violent video games. Hum Brain Mapp 27:948–956
McCall C, Blascovich J, Young A, Persky S (2009) Proxemic behaviors as predictors of aggression towards Black (but not White) males in an immersive virtual environment. Soc Influence 4(2):138–154
McDermott D (2007) Artificial intelligence and consciousness. In: Zelazo PD, Moscovitch M, Thompson E (eds) The Cambridge handbook of consciousness. Cambridge University Press, Cambridge, pp 117–150
Meehan M, Insko B, Whitton M, Brooks FP (2002) Physiological measures of presence in stressful virtual environments. ACM Trans Graph Proc ACM SIGGRAPH 21(3):645–653
Möller I, Krahé B (2009) Exposure to violent video games and aggression in German adolescents. Aggress Behav 35:75–89
Paik H, Comstock G (1994) The effects of television violence on antisocial behavior: a meta-analysis. Commun Res 21:516–546
Pizarro DA, Detweiler-Bedell B, Bloom P (2006) The creativity of everyday moral reasoning: empathy, disgust and moral persuasion. In: Kaufman J, Baer J (eds) Creativity and reason in cognitive development. Cambridge University Press, Cambridge, pp 81–98
Powers TM (2003) Real wrongs in virtual communities. Ethics Inf Technol 5:191–198
Ray TS (1992) An approach to the synthesis of life. In: Langton CG, Taylor C, Farmer JD, Rasmussen S (eds) Artificial life II. Addison-Wesley, Redwood City, pp 371–408
Roseman IJ (2001) A model of appraisal in the emotion system. In: Scherer K, Schorr A, Johnstone T (eds) Appraisal processes in emotion. Theory, methods, research. Oxford University Press, New York, pp 68–91
Searle JR (1980) Minds, brains, and programs. Behav Brain Sci 3:417–457
Searle J (1990) Is the brain's mind a computer program? Sci Am 262:26–31
Shapiro MA, McDonald DG (1992) I'm not a real doctor, but I play one in virtual reality: implications of virtual reality for judgments about reality. J Commun 42:94–114
Slater MD, Henry KL, Swaim RC, Anderson LL (2003) Violent media content aggressiveness in adolescents. Commun Res 30(6):713–736
Smith ER, DeCoster J (2000) Dual process models in social and cognitive psychology: conceptual integration and links to underlying memory systems. Pers Soc Psychol Rev 4:108–131
Spafford EH (1989) Computer viruses as artificial life. Manuscript retrieved online from http://www.scs.carleton.ca/~soma/biosec/readings/spafford-viruses.pdf, accessed on August 3, 2010
Suler JR, Phillips W (1998) The bad boys of cyberspace: deviant behavior in multimedia chat communities. Cyberpsychol Behav 1:275–294
Weber M (1919) Politik als Beruf [Politics as a vocation]. Büchergilde Gutenberg, Frankfurt am Main
Weber R, Ritterfeld U, Mathiak K (2006) Does playing violent video games induce aggression? Empirical evidence of a functional magnetic resonance imaging study. Media Psychol 8(1): 39–60
Whang LS-M, Chang G (2004) Lifestyles of virtual world residents: living in the on-line game "lineage". Cyberpsychol Behav 7(5):592–600
Wolfendale J (2007) My avatar, my self: virtual harm and attachment. Ethics Inf Technol 9:111–119
Yee N, Bailenson JN, Ducheneaut N (2009) The Proteus effect: implications of transformed digital self-representation on online and offline behavior. Commun Res 36(2):285–312
Zillmann D (2006) Dramaturgy for emotions from fictional narration. In: Bryant J, Vorderer P (eds) Psychology of entertainment. Lawrence Erlbaum, Mahwah, pp 215–238

Media Violence and Criminality

Dieter Hermann

Abstract In the research on effects of media, the question on the influence of media on real violence is of great importance. Numerous empirical studies give the impression that reliable findings exist; however, almost all investigations are cross-sectional studies or laboratory experiments. Cross-sectional studies have the disadvantage that causal structures are only shown insufficiently; laboratory experiments have the disadvantage that only short-term effects are registered. Meta-analyses show that both methods lead to gradually different results. Panel studies and natural experiments which can model causal effects correctly have so far been made only rarely. The results of the studies confirm the hypothesis that the consumption of media violence and violent acting correspond. Despite methodological deficits the empirical facts seem to be unambiguous; the theoretical interpretation is problematic. In the relevant empirical studies on this subject, the approach of the learning theory is of central importance. Media contents are seen as models accepted by recipients. Taking this as a background, the results of empirical studies can be interpreted in such a way that the consumption of media violence is one cause of real violence. Assuming, however, other crime and action theories, the empirical results can also be interpreted in such a way that the consumption of media violence and violent acting has common causes and that the correspondence between the characteristics is a spurious correlation. As a result it must be stated that there is a research deficit concerning the question of the influence of media on real violence.

D. Hermann (✉)
Institute of Criminology, University of Heidelberg, Heidelberg, Germany
e-mail: hermann@krimi.uni-heidelberg.de

K. Cornelius and D. Hermann (eds.), *Virtual Worlds and Criminality*,
DOI 10.1007/978-3-642-20823-2_4, © Springer-Verlag Berlin Heidelberg 2011

1 Introduction

There are a high number of publications on the research on effects of media – Groebel and Gleich (1993) as well as Kunczik and Zipfel (2002) estimate the number of relevant studies to be 5,000, which come from different fields treating this subject: criminology and criminal sociology, media and communication sociology, election sociology and market research and psychology. There is a difference in terminology depending on the specific fields; the articles are published in different journals and, most of all, only articles of the particular discipline are cited so that, as far as it can be seen to date, there is no interdisciplinary overall result yet. In addition, the results of empirical studies on the influence of violence in media on violent action are contradictory. Only the press always gives a homogeneous idea when the stimulating effect of media violence is apparently proven by spectacular individual cases.

It is very difficult to take stock of empirical investigations on the influence of media consumption on violence due to different study conceptions: Qualitative studies can only partly be compared with quantitative studies, experiments only to some extent with surveys and studies with individual data hardly with aggregate data investigations. In addition, different operationalisations of media violence, the consideration of different investigation populations and differences in statistical models to estimate the media effect make a comparison more difficult since the differences in the type of investigation also cause differences in extent and generalisability of results. Due to the high number of studies, this article refers particular to reviews and meta-analyses, i.e. to studies which combine the results of several studies. Since the studies mainly come from the USA, some new single studies from Germany shall additionally be taken into consideration.

In a further step, the results of empirical investigations are compared with hypotheses from theories suitable to explain violent crime. This helps to theoretically reflect empirical results since causality can be tested only partially by empirical methods. For a discussion of the causality question dealing with the relation between media consumption and violent acting a confrontation of empirical studies with theories is necessary.

2 Investigation Methods and Their Limitations

As a rule, studies on the effects of media are made as surveys or laboratory experiments. These methods allow taking into consideration the unreported aggressive behaviour (dark field) and not only activities registered by the police or by law agencies. Studies with reported violence always bear the risk that their results depend on strategies of handling by the official control authorities; thus, dark field studies are, as a rule, more valid than bright field data. Surveys and laboratory experiments are usually dark field studies; they relate to the individual level – the objects examined are people. Studies on the macro level, however, are based on bright field data where crime rates for selected offences are linked to media violence.

Consequently, the results of empirical studies on the effects of media can only partly be compared with bright and dark field data as well as studies on micro and macro level. This also holds for experiments and surveys. The advantage of laboratory experiments compared to surveys is the good consideration of frame conditions; however, the transferability of results to non-experimental situations remains open. In addition, laboratory experiments can only measure short-time effects and an extrapolation to a longer space of time is afflicted with uncertainties. The hypothesis that an intensive reception of media violence over a longer period of time has an influence on the behaviour of the recipient can hardly be verified under laboratory conditions, and the hypothesis that the consumption of media violence is relevant for any kind of action immediately after reception cannot be tested by surveys.

The advantages of surveys compared to laboratory experiments are that they usually have a higher number of cases and can register violent acting in a relatively differentiated manner. Experiments, on the other hand, in most cases only register the aggressiveness of a game situation. However, the measurement of violent acting by surveys is only valid restrictedly because it must be expected that its extent and severity are underestimated (Hermann and Weninger 1999). The estimated values of measures of association are assumed to be too low so that an incorrect acceptance of hypotheses of association cannot be expected due to the measurement problems shown. In addition, these measurement problems apply to all individuals in a survey, independent of an intensive or low consumption of media violence. While comparing groups with low and high consumption of media violence it cannot be expected that the deficits in measurement quality shown lead to a considerable bias of investigation results.

With cross-sectional surveys, media consumption and violent acting are measured retrospectively. Thus, in statistical analyses, cause and effect cannot be distinguished (from each other) such that in measures of association both causal directions are taken into consideration, i.e. the influence of the media consumption on violence and the influence of violent orientation on media consumption. This problem is less serious with panel studies; these, however, can only partially solve the problem. Even if the consumption of media violence was registered before the measurement of violent acting and both correlate with each other, it cannot be concluded that media consumption is relevant for action. It could also be possible that media consumption of violence and the respective acting are a consequence of a violence orientation which is long-term stable such that, in the end, only a spurious correlation is registered. This problem can only be solved by a model taking these third variables into consideration.

3 Empirical Studies

3.1 Individual Studies

Field experiments were possible only for a short time after the implementation of television. These studies were, as far as it can be seen, not realised in Germany.

The study of Joy et al. (1986) is one of the few existing field experiments. In this study, the authors observed the extent of physical and verbal aggression of children in three small Canadian cities which were differentiated by the reception of TV channels: One community had no channel at all, the second only one and the third several channels. The observations were repeated 2 years after TV had been introduced in the community that, up to then, had no channel at all, and the result was a significant increase in aggression only in this community. According to this, the confrontation with TV broadcasts seems to promote aggression.

Grimm (1999, 2000) has conducted several laboratory experiments on media effect research. In the first experiment, 186 test persons between 11 and 65 years – the average age was 22 – were shown clips from different martial arts films like "Karate Tiger" and "Bloodsport". Before this they had to complete a questionnaire about their aggression, their understanding of violence, their readiness for violence and other subjects. The test persons were divided into four groups which saw different film clips where the scenes of the films varied in the type of the violence shown. In martial arts scenes with "clean" violence the fights were according to rules and in most cases without damage to the opponent, whereas the scenes with "dirty" violence were much more brutal and caused the death of the opponent. Physiological measurements – pulse frequency and conductivity of the dermis – were made during the presentation of the film, and after the presentation the psychosocial characteristics were measured again by the questionnaire already used before.

In the total sample, the film consumption led to a significant decrease of the self-estimated aggression potential and a significant increase of fear, this increase of fear being the consequence, in first place, of the consumption of film scenes with dirty violence. The highest decrease of aggression was found in the group who had first been confronted with dirty and then with clean violence.

In another experiment, Grimm (1999, 2000) has examined gender-specific differences in the effects of consumption of media violence. 92 test persons aged between 12 and 60 – the average age was 20 – were divided into three groups of almost the same size. These were shown trailers of the film "Savage Street – Street of Violence" in different order. In one part of the film a woman is the offender and a man the victim,[1] in another vice versa.[2] When the films were shown in this order, the women showed extreme reactions of fear; their aggression, however, remained unchanged whereas it decreased with the male recipients. When the films were

[1]The scene starts in a bathroom. Brenda takes a bath, towels herself off, dresses herself and waits – armed with bow and arrow – for Jake who then arrives with a pistol. Brenda, however, hits him with two arrows. Jake cries out loud and shoots out blindly without hitting anybody. However, he attacks Brenda. They are struggling hard and Jake is hurt by a knife in the belly. Brenda then empties a bucket of paint over him and sets light to him. Jack burns alive.

[2]In a second scene, men are the offenders and a woman is the victim. There is a young woman buying a wedding dress. Finding out that four young men follow her, she runs away. The dramatic hunt goes through a tunnel and upstairs to a bridge. There, the pursuers surround her, kill her without observable motive and throw her off the bridge.

shown in the inverse order, this led to an increase in aggression and readiness for violence with men.

All in all, these laboratory experiments show that short-term consequences of media violence depend on the recipient himself as well as on the way it is shown in a film and the content of violent scenes. Media effects seem to be complex and can hardly be shown by a simple stimulus reaction model.

Scheungrab (1993) has examined the question on the relation between media consumption and violence with a survey among 50 young people and adolescents in prison and 51 not in prison. The data of the comparative sample were registered in the frame of the diploma theses of Mayer (1992) and Wild (1992). Both theses used almost the same sampling instrument, a conversation guide realised in the form of problem-centred qualitative interviews. The two samples consisted only of men. The imprisoned persons came from two Bavarian prisons; Mayer (1992) interviewed apprentices and Wild (1992) members of ice hockey fan clubs from Regensburg and Straubing. The average age of the imprisoned sample was 18.5 years, the test persons of the other group were, on average, 1 year younger. The differences in the original social stratum could be neglected. Media consumption and delinquency rate were registered by self reports.

The qualitative data have been quantified for the statistical analysis. The results of the analysis are unambiguous: The consumption of media violence influences delinquency and vice versa. An increase in consumption of violent acts and, especially, horror films means an increase in delinquency – and vice versa. This means, that the frequency of the consumption of media violence and especially the consumption of horror films has an influence on criminal activities, and vice versa. In addition, preferences for this kind of films as well as the reception of videos, indexed films and horror films, the degree of conviction of the feasibility of the delinquent techniques shown in the media are relevant factors for delinquency. The frequency of watching videos and indexed films also influences the acceptance of neutralising techniques which can be seen in these kinds of films. All effects mentioned are significant. Altogether, especially horror and indexed films are in a complex interdependental relation. Delinquent behaviour is not only a simple imitation of media criminality but also, probably, resulting from interdependental mechanisms: The consumption of violence-related media changes the conviction of feasibility of delinquent techniques shown in films as well as the acceptance of medially transmitted neutralising techniques – and theses characteristics are finally decisive for the use of violence.

The interview study of Gentile et al. (2004) especially deals with the influence of video games on violence. They interviewed 607 thirteen- to fifteen-year-old male and female pupils in the United States. According to a path analysis, the frequency of violent video games played by these pupils and the intensity of violence of the games has significant effects on the number of assaults. The standardised path coefficient is, however, only 0.07. The question of how long the games had been played has, however, no influence on this behaviour.

Raithel (2003) also studied the influence of video games on violence, but he additionally took other media into consideration such that of this study effects of video games and film consumption could be compared with each other. In a survey of 436 male and female pupils, he examined the correlation between media consumption and violent delinquency. The interviewed persons were between 15 and 18 years old and attended secondary schools in Bamberg. Violent crimes were registered by the question of whether within the last 12 months an offence of robbery or bodily harm – with or without weapon – had been committed. The results of multiple regression analysis showed that especially bodily harm without weapon can be explained by the intensity of the use of certain computer games, especially ego shooter and martial arts games: The standardised partial regression coefficient is above 0.5. Compared to this, the consumption of violence-related films (horror, war, battle and action films as well as crime films) only played a subordinate role. For bodily harms with weapon, the causal mechanisms are vice versa: Especially the consumption of aggressive films highly corresponds with the commission of this offence ($\beta = 0.4$), computer games are, compared to this, only of marginal importance. With robbery offences, too, only the consumption of films ($\beta = 0.3$) and not the use of computer games is associated with the commission of the offence. The author assumes that the occupation with violence-accentuated computer games and films can be interpreted as the expression of a certain lifestyle. From a measurement-theoretical point of view this can be understood in a way that the preference for media violence is a lifestyle having several indicators, i.e. the occupation with violent games and the consumption of violent films. If, however, both characteristics are measurements of a single latent variable, the multiple regressions with both indicators as independent variables would lead to biased estimations. Both are dependent on each other and measure the same construct (Lieberson 1985, p 120f). Thus, the results of Raithel (2003, p. 293) indicating that the standardised partial regression coefficients vary offence-specifically for the different forms of media consumption must be interpreted under reserve. The central result – media consumption has an influence on delinquency – is probably not affected by this.

The works of Huesmann et al. (1997) as well as Huesmann and Moise (1998) are based on two panel studies. The first survey started in 1977 and covered interviews with approximately 750 boys and girls from Chicago aged 6–8. In the last survey wave from 1992 to 1994, more than 300 persons could be taken into consideration. The correlation coefficients between the extent of consumption of TV violence of the interviewed children and the verbal and physical aggression of the same persons at adult age were approximately 0.2 for the male as well as for the female participants. When only physical aggression was taken into consideration in the analysis, the coefficients were a bit smaller. The values are significant, and the effects could also be confirmed with a statistical control of stratum, intelligence quotient, sex and aggression level at first wave. Reversed, the aggression of the interviewed children has no significant influence on the increase of media violence consumption.

The second study of Huesmann and colleagues is based on data of the Columbia County Longitudinal Study where, in 1960, every child of the third classes of all Columbia County schools had been interviewed, almost 900 persons. The average

age then was 8 years. The following investigations were made at the age of 19, 30 and 48, whereas the last wave was not included in the media effect analysis. As a whole, 285 persons were interviewed in all waves. In this study, too, an influence of the consumption of media violence in the childhood on the aggression in the adulthood could be shown. Especially the respective media consumption at the time of the first wave had effects on aggression in the following waves, independent of intelligence quotient, sex and the original aggression level of the persons interviewed.

Another panel study was conducted by Johnson et al. (2002). In 1975, they interviewed 707 children from randomly selected families in two New York Counties aged between 1 and 10 years. The average age of the first wave was 6, in the following waves 14, 16, 22 and 30 years. According to the results of the study, the situation in the childhood (first wave) influences the extent of later TV consumption (second wave): Socially neglected and mentally conspicuous children from lower classes having grown up in insecure neighbourhoods spent significantly more time watching TV then others. The extent of the TV consumption of the interviewed at the time of the second wave significantly corresponds to their aggression and violence in the next waves. Especially serious is the difference between those watching few and those watching much TV among male young people who already had a relatively high aggression potential in the second wave: Among those persons watching less than 1 h per day TV, the prevalence rate for aggressive behaviour in the two following waves was less than 10%; if, however, they spent more than 3 h a day in front of the TV, the respective value was above 60%. But also among the non-aggressive male young people the aggression rate varies significantly depending on the duration of earlier TV consumption. For female young persons, the relation between consumption intensity and aggression is not significant. The results vary only marginally when variables like the degree of social neglect during childhood, degree of insecurity in the neighbourhood, level of the family income, style of education by the parents, mental conspicuousness in childhood and earlier aggression are controlled.

Brosius, Esser and Scheufele (Brosius and Esser 1995; Esser et al. 2002) have conducted empirical studies with aggregated data on the question of imitation of offences which have been reported on in the media. The question was whether the reporting on xenophobic offences, especially arson attacks on homes for asylum seekers, was only a reaction to the respective offence or whether the respective media reporting lead to an increase of offences. The authors checked these relations for several periods of time. On the basis of data on the development of immigration numbers, population opinions, media coverage and offences, Brosius and Esser (1995) develop an escalation model of violence. The results have been achieved especially by linking content analyses of newspaper reports and TV news on xenophobic offences on the one hand with data of the Police Criminal Statistics on xenophobic and extreme right-wing offences on the other hand – these were weekly prepared data of the Federal Criminal Offices from six federal states. By the determination of time-lagged correlations the hypothesis on the relation between media reporting and offences could be tested, a check of both causal directions being possible: offences can be seen as a consequence of reporting and reporting can be seen as a reaction to offences. For the analysis, the authors divided the survey period ranging from August 1990 to July 1993 into two phases. The first phase up to September 1992 was characterised by a continuously growing number of violent offences, especially by assassinations in the new German states in former Eastern Germany (Hoyerswerda, Rostock). In the second phase, the number of assassinations has increased dramatically, among others in Mölln and Solingen (old German states).

In the first phase, the relation between media reporting and the extent of xenophobic violence is especially distinctive. The extent of xenophobic violence increased significantly approximately 1 week after corresponding media reports. The correlation between the number of reports on xenophobic offences and the number of respective offences committed in the week thereafter was 0.6 and was significant. They came to the conclusion that especially the reflex-type reaction of the whole media system on especially violent key events (Hoyerswerda, Rostock, Mölln and Solingen) has led to a high number of imitation offences (Brosius): The reporting on the events mentioned contributed to the suggestive–imitative spread of violence.

In the second phase, the type of media reporting on these kinds of offences changed, and protest actions against xenophobia were organised by the population. In this period, the highest correlation between media reporting and delinquency can be found when both characteristics have been registered at the same time – there are, thus, no more imitation effects.

Esser et al. (2002) continued the analysis on the relation between media reporting and violence. There was no imitating effect of media reports in the time between August 1993 and December 1995. The reports mostly covered the situation as investigated by the BKA (Bundeskriminalamt, Federal Bureau of Investigation). Also from January until December 1996, there were no distinctive patterns in the time-lag correlations when all xenophobic offences were taken into consideration in the media analysis. If, however, the frequency of xenophobic offences registered by the police is linked with the frequency of reports on the violence of Kurds and their political party PKK, this leads to time-lag correlations which are higher than 0.6 according to the focus of the preceding media reporting. In 1996, there were some illegal and violent demonstrations of Kurds and PKK supporters, and just in July the PKK committed more than 50 arson attacks against Turkish facilities. The more often newspapers described the Kurds as extreme violent offenders, the more xenophobic violence seemed to exist. The latency phase was 2–4 weeks.

The authors continued their survey for the time period between January and December 2000. From June on, the number of media reports on xenophobic and extreme right-wing offences has increased significantly, and for this period an effect can be seen, however, only for the BILD (a famous German yellow press paper). The more often there were reports on a ban on the NDP (right-wing National Democratic Party) and sanctions against the NPD, the higher was the number of extreme right-wing offences with a delay of approximately 1 week ($r = 0.4$). There could not be found any further relations.

As a whole, media reporting – under certain social conditions – seems to lead to criminal reactions especially when these reports have a provoking character for some groups of people.

3.2 Reviews and Meta Analyses

According to Groebel and Gleich (2004), the majority of the approximately 5,000 studies on media violence published so far discovered an aggression-increasing effect, although this was very often low. Only few studies found no aggression-blocking effects. Felson (1996) comes to a similar result in a literature review: Sporadic watching of violence-related media contents seems to have no consequences, but with intensive consumption combined with unfavourable frame conditions like deviant friends, conflicts with parents or an aggressive basic attitude, the influence of media consumption on violence can be seen clearly, this effect being greater in laboratory than in field studies.

Paik and Comstock (1994) conducted a meta-analysis of 217 studies from the years 1957 to 1990 on TV violence and antisocial behaviour. A total of 1,142 hypotheses on this subject were tested in these studies. Approximately 58% of the hypothesis tests confirmed a positive correlation: The higher the reception of media violence, the more distinct is antisocial behaviour, 8% of the hypotheses show a negative relation and in approximately 33% of the studies, no association can be proved. Combining all studies, the correlation coefficient between consumption of violent-related TV broadcasts and antisocial behaviour is $r = 0.31$. The size of the association measure depends on the type of the study. For laboratory experiments, the correlation is $r = 0.40$, and for surveys, $r = 0.19$. All coefficients mentioned are highly significant. Gender differences mainly appear in experiments. Independent of the study design, the correlation coefficient between consumption of TV violence and antisocial behaviour is $r = 0.26$ for women and $r = 0.36$ for men. Based on the assumption that experiments mainly register short-term effects and surveys long-term effects and interrelationships, the meta-analysis can be summarised as follows: The consumption of TV violence has a significant short-term effect on antisocial behaviour especially among men. Taking a longer period of time, the association is less significant.

Sherry's (2001) meta-analysis is restricted to experiments on video games and aggression. About 25 studies from 1975 to 2000 were taken into consideration. In most of the experiments, a treatment group consumed violent-related and a control group non-violent video games. The video games in the experimental phase took between 5 and 75 min. Aggression was measured by different procedures: Aggression while attending the experiment, personal question on the readiness for aggression and written questions on the existence of aggressive feelings. The test persons in the studies taken into consideration were aged between 4 and 34, the largest part of the study was, however, restricted to young people. The number of cases per study varied between 14 and 278. Almost all studies found a relation between type of the video game and aggression. The unweighted medium correlation coefficient between video games and aggression was $r = 0.16$: Test persons who played violent video games were more aggressive than the others. The value is highly significant and varies only negligible when weighting the case number. In addition, the effect of video games depends on the type of violence dominating the games. With violent-related sports, video games, the association with aggression is the lowest, it is higher with games including violence against persons or with fantasy games. In addition, the size of the correlation coefficient in the studies taken into consideration can be explained relatively well by the time of the study ($r = 0.39$): The more current the study, the higher the correlation coefficient.

Bushman and Anderson (2001) as well as Anderson and Bushman (2002) present the results of a comprehensive meta-analysis. For this purpose, they have selected all relevant studies up to the year 2000 from the literature database PsycINFO, taking into consideration only studies linking media consumption to aggressive behaviour. As a consequence, they have excluded studies treating only aggressive attitudes, readiness for violence or unsocial behaviour. About 202 studies with different samples have been taken into consideration in the meta-analysis. The biggest part of the surveys, i.e. 85%, was conducted in 1970 and later.

A central result of the studies is that the correlation between consumption of media violence and violent acting depends on the time the survey was conducted. The more current the study is, the higher is the found correlation coefficient. In addition, the results of the studies on media effects depend on the study design. The degree of the relation between the corresponding media consumption and violence is higher with experimental studies than with nonexperimental studies. With growing actuality of the studies, however, the differences decrease. The results are shown in Fig. 1.

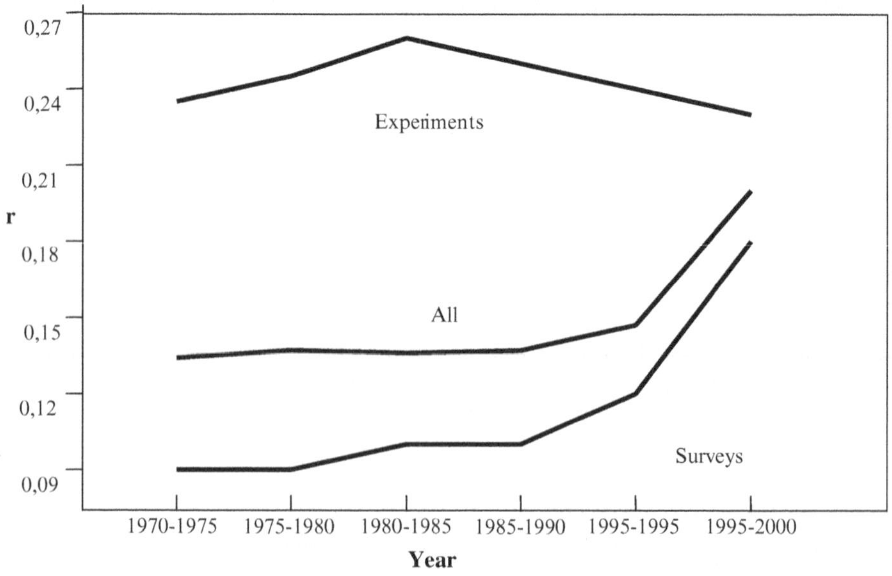

Fig. 1 The dependency of the correlation between consumption of media violence and violent acting on the time of publication of the study and on the study design Data from Bushman and Anderson (2001, p. 484)

The correlation coefficient between publication dates of the studies and effect sizes for the consumption of media violence is 0.4, if all 202 studies are taken into consideration; this value is significantly different from zero. The corresponding correlation for experiments is, however, not significant – opposite to the interview studies. The increase in effect sizes could have its cause in an increase in quality of the interview studies since the methods of sample census and the methods of statistical analysis have improved. Another cause could be that the media consumption has become more and more important and that, at least in parts of the society, the reception of media violence has increased such that long-term media effects become more obvious. The difference in the estimation of media effects between experiments and interviews are explained by Bushman and Anderson by the better controllability of independent variables in experiments, by a shorter time period between media consumption and measurement of effects as well as by – compared to the media violence consumed in daily life – higher intensity of media violence in experimental situations. However, the differences could also be explained by the number of cases. Generally, significantly fewer cases are taken into consideration with experiments than with interviews, and the number of cases has an influence on the size of association measures.

3.3 Conclusion of Empirical Studies

As a whole, there are numerous empirical studies on the relation between media consumption and violence. The results vary significantly. There exist, however, some clear trends:

New meta-analyses on the subject show obvious results: The more current the study, the greater the relation between consumption of media violence and violent acting.

Panel studies show that media consumption at a young age corresponds with aggression at adult age, especially with men.

The media effects in laboratory experiments are higher than in interview studies. This can be interpreted in a way that short-term effects are higher than long-term effects.

The extensiveness and the type of media consumption depend on the social conditions of the family.

4 The Relation Between Media Consumption and Violence from the Perspective of Crime Theories

The focus of the criminological media effect research treats the question whether and how the reception of media violence leads to violent acting. This subject can be assigned to aetiological crime studies, since these shall give answers to the question on the cause of crime and, thus, of violent crime. It is thus consequent to derive hypotheses on the influence of the consumption of violence in media on violent acting from the existing crime theories. This is realised here exemplarily for three crime theories. Although the media consumption plays a subordinate role in most crime theories or is not directly involved at all, an extension of the existing theories by this question is possible. Thus the empirically often confirmed correlation between media consumption and violence can be interpreted theoretically at different manners. For this reason, some crime theories will be presented in short and applied to the question on the relation between medially transmitted violence and violent acting.

Sutherland's (1979) theory of differential association is a classical theory to explain criminal acting. According to this theory, criminality is the consequence of a corresponding attitude which is learned especially by contacts with criminals and mostly in personal groups. One important mechanism is the operant conditioning. According to this, the frequency of criminal behaviour is higher if this behaviour has been remunerated and not punished in the past. However, the subjective evaluation of the acting person is decisive for the classification of remuneration and punishment as reactions to criminality. According to such a learning theory, it can be postulated that these learning processes can also be triggered by media consumption. A hypothesis can be as follows: The more often positively evaluated and remunerated media violence is received, the higher is the probability of violent acting.

According to Bandura (1968, 1979), aggressive behaviour is learned, but, compared to the Stimulus-Response-Theory, he uses a more complex approach and takes cognitive processes into consideration. Observed actions, whether real or virtual, are memorised as models for own acting. The realisation of these models depends on several conditions, especially on the remuneration the acting person has experienced, on the cognitive valuation of the model acting by the recipient and on his ability for self-control. "Not everything that is learned will be realised. Discrepancies between things learned and their realisation will occur especially when the things learned only have a minor functional value or have a high risk of punishment – and thus adverse behavioural consequences" (Merten 1999, p. 43). According to this hypothesis, the consumption of media violence leads to real violence if certain personal and situative conditions are fulfilled. Figure 2 shows the postulated relation graphically.

According to Hirschi's (1969) Control Theory, delinquency is explained by lacking external and internal control. By socialisation processes the human being

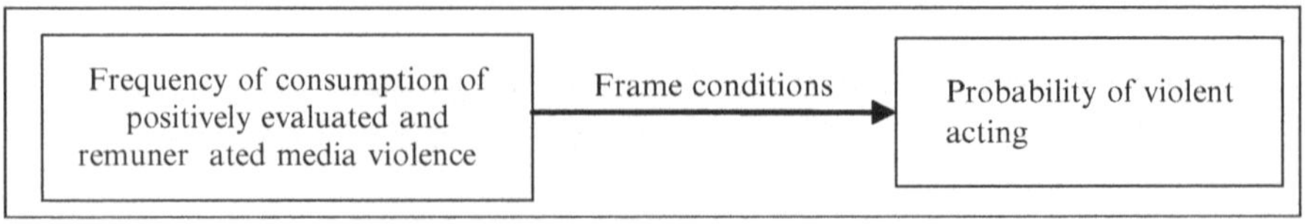

Fig. 2 Hypothetic causal structure on the influence of media consumption on violence according to learning-theories

must learn to restrict his freedom, which includes the freedom to act according to his wishes and to commit offences. The success of the process depends on four factors: the attachment by personal relations, the commitment to social roles, the organisational involvement in institutions and conventional activities and the faith in the liability of conventional moral standards and beliefs. The stronger these four elements are developed, the less is the probability to commit offences.

Gottfredson and Hirschi (1990) developed this approach to a theory of self-control. This must be understood as rational weighting of costs and benefits of an action where also long-term aspects must be taken into consideration. Criminality is characterised by a short-term benefit but, in the long term, by relatively high costs. If a person overemphasises the short-term advantages and only inadequately considers the long-term costs, delinquent acting and other forms of deviant behaviour are more probable than with a person with realistic cost-benefit-estimation of delinquent behaviour. The development of self-control as well as the above-mentioned aspects of attachment and commitment should, according to this theory, mostly take place within the family during the childhood phase.

The intensive consumption of media violence does, utilitaristically, not differ from criminality – in both cases, benefit can be reached on the short term and costs develop on the long term. Thus, an insufficient degree of self-control would either increase delinquent behaviour or consumption of media violence. According to this model, the relation between (violent) delinquency and media violence is a spurious correlation. The hypotheses are shown graphically in Fig. 3.

According to the voluntaristic crime theory of Hermann (2003, 2008), criminality is, primarily, a consequence of certain value orientations. The basis is a theory of action. The acting person is seen as subject setting oneself a target and being productively reality managing and being integrated into a complex environment. The situation of the acting person is characterised by his social structural position and by the means he has to reach his targets. Internalised values and norms have the function to select the subjectively important; this does not only concern targets but also the means to reach these targets. Furthermore values have the function to

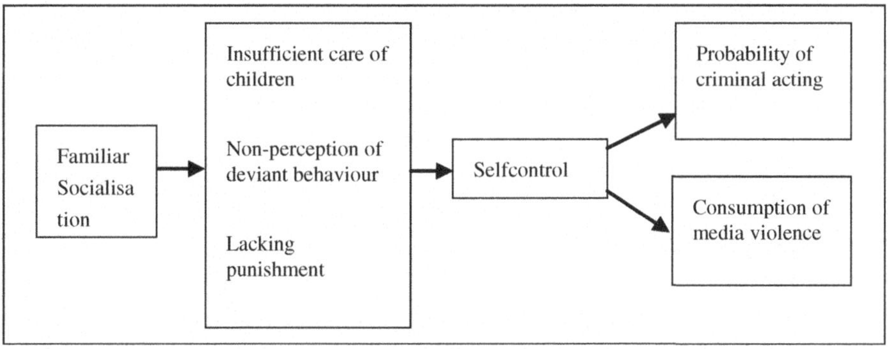

Fig. 3 Hypothetical causal structure on the influence of media consumption on criminality according to the Control Theory of Gottfredson and Hirschi

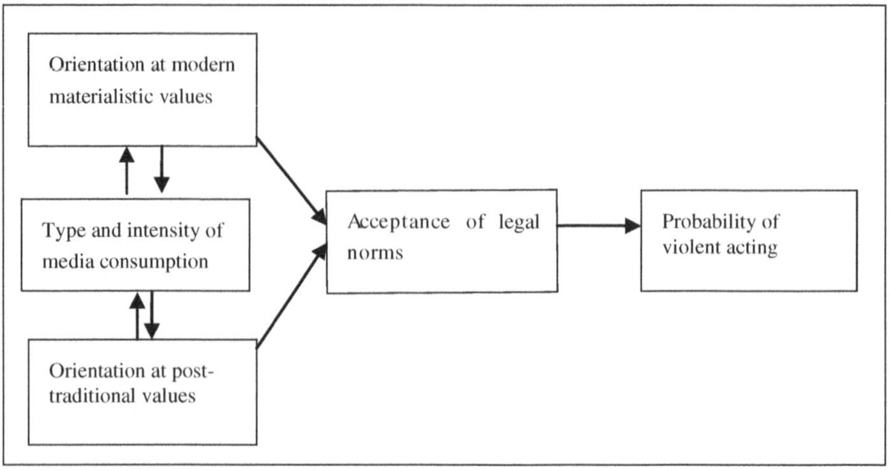

Fig. 4 Hypothetic causal structure on the influence of media consumption on criminality according to the voluntaristic theory of crime

reduce the complexity environment. Prior to each action, a selection must be made from the variety of possible targets and means; in addition and in most cases, the complexity of the situation must be reduced – the selection instruments for this are values and norms. Relevant causes for criminality are (1) the orientation at post-traditional values, i.e. at a norm-oriented achievement ethics, a conservative conformism and a religious orientation, (2) the orientation at modern materialistic values, i.e. subcultural materialistic values and hedonistic values and, (3) the acceptance of legal norms. These value orientations are the cause of norm acceptance. The norms and values of an individual do not only depend on his structural situation but are also interrelated with norms and values of environment systems, those include peer group and world of media.

According to this theory it can be assumed that, on the long term, the media consumption influences the value orientations of a person – and, vice versa, that the value orientations of a person influence his media consumption. Thus, criminality would not be a direct consequence of media reception but a direct effect of value orientations influenced by the media, and the media consumption itself depends on the values of the recipient. The hypotheses are shown in Fig. 4.

5 Consequences

The empirical studies on media effect research have method-specific deficits, but with an overall view on the studies it is possible to draw a balance under reserve. Due to the meta-analyses, a relation between the consumption of violent media and violent acting can be assumed as being probable. The bigger part of the studies has been conducted in the USA where – due to a very high media presence – the relation between media violence consumption and violent action can be looked at as being significant. This association seems to depend on the extent to which media is offered and confrontation with media violence. Due to the media expansion, the extent of the relation has probably increased in recent years.

Another result of the media effect studies is that media consumption does not automatically and not in all cases lead to violence. Women and men, for example, seem to react differently to media violence such that it can be assumed that socialisation results influence the effect of media reception.

Due to the results of the panel studies, a causal relation between the consumption of media violence and violent acting can be assumed, since an association can also be proven when the media consumption has taken place long before criminal acts. Not clear are, however, the causal transmission mechanisms and the frame conditions for the occurrence of media effects – this is a deficit of the theoretical modelling. Thus, the empirical results must be interpreted differently on the basis of learning theory, the control theory and the voluntaristic theory of crime. According to the learning theory, the relation between the consumption of media violence and violent acting must be interpreted causally, according to the control theory of Gottfredson and Hirschi a spurious correlation must be assumed and according to the voluntaristic theory of crime, the media consumption has an influence on the value socialisation and influences the probability of violent delinquency via the value orientations. A further conclusion is that media consumption is influenced by value orientations. Thus, a research deficit can be stated in the question on the influence of media violence on real violence. Theory-comparing panel studies are required.

References

Anderson CA, Bushman BJ (2002) Media violence and the American public revisited. Am Psychol 57:448–450

Bandura A (1968) What television violence can do to your child. In: Larson ON (ed) Violence and the mass media. Harper and Row, New York, pp 123–130

Bandura A (1979) Aggression: eine sozial-lerntheoretische analyse. Klett-Cotta, Stuttgart

Brosius H-B, o.J. Zwischen Eskalation und Verantwortung. Die Berichterstattung über fremdenfeindliche Gewalt und Rechtsextremismus. http://www.mediageneration.net/jugendszene/buch15.pdf (Stand 06/2009)

Brosius H-B, Esser F (1995) Eskalation durch Berichterstattung? Westdeutscher Verlag, Opladen

Bushman BJ, Anderson CA (2001) Media violence and the american public. Scientific facts versus media misinformation. Am Psychol 56:477–489

Esser F, Scheufele B, Brosius H-B (2002) Fremdenfeindlichkeit als Medienthema und Medienwirkung. Westdeutscher Verlag, Wiesbaden

Felson RB (1996) Mass media effects on violent behavior. Annu Rev Sociol 22:103–128

Gentile DA, Lynch PA, Linder JR, Walsh DA (2004) The effects of violent video game habits on adolescent hostility, aggressive behaviors, and school performance. J Adolesc 27:5–22

Gottfredson MR, Hirschi T (1990) A general theory of crime. Stanford University Press, Stanford

Grimm J (1999) Fernsehgewalt. Zuwendungsattraktivität – Erregungsverläufe – sozialer Effekt. Zur Begründung und praktischen Anwendung eines kognitiv-physiologischen Ansatzes der Medienwirkungsforschung am Beispiel von Gewaltdarstellungen. Westdeutscher Verlag, Opladen

Grimm J (2000) Mediengewalt – Wirkungen jenseits von Imitationen. Zum Einfluss ästhetischer und dramaturgischer Faktoren auf die Aggressionsvermittlung. In: Bergmann S (ed) Mediale Gewalt – eine reale Bedrohung für Kinder? Gesellschaft für Medienpädagogik und Kommunikationskultur und Internetpublikation, Bielefeld, pp 40–50. http://www.mediengewalt.de/_arc/pdf/grimm_imitation.pdf (Stand: 06/2009).

Groebel J, Gleich U (1993) Gewaltprofil des deutschen Fernsehprogramms. Eine Analyse des Angebots privater und öffentlich-rechtlicher Sender. Leske + Budrich, Opladen

Groebel J, Gleich U (2004) Medien und Gewalt. http://www.jott-we-de.de/infosozial/data/gewalt.html (Stand: 06/2009)

Hermann D (2003) Werte und Kriminalität. Konzeption einer allgemeinen Kriminalitätstheorie. VS Verlag für Sozialwissenschaften, Wiesbaden

Hermann D (2008) Posttraditionale Ethik. Empirische Analysen und theoretische Reflexionen. Merus, Hamburg

Hermann D, Weninger W (1999) Das Dunkelfeld in Dunkelfelduntersuchungen. Über die Messung selbstberichteter Delinquenz. Kölner Z Soziologie Sozialpsychologie 51:759–766

Hirschi T (1969) Causes of delinquency. University of California Press, Berkeley

Huesmann LR, Moise J (1998) The stability and continuity of aggression from early childhood to young adulthood. In: Flannery DJ, Huff CR (eds) Youth violence: prevention, intervention, and social policy. American Psychiatric Press, Washington, pp 73–95

Huesmann LR, Moise J, Podolski CL (1997) The effects of media violence on the development of antisocial behaviour. In: Stoff D, Breiling J, Maser J (eds) Handbook of antisocial behavior. Wiley, New York, pp 181–193

Johnson JG, Cohen P, Smailes EM, Kasen S, Brook JS (2002) Television viewing and aggressive behavior during adolescence and adulthood. Science 295:2468–2474

Joy LA, Kimball MM, Zabrack ML (1986) Television and children's aggressive behavior. In: Williams TM (ed) The impact of television: a natural experiment in three communities. Academic, Orlando, pp 303–360

Kunczik M, Zipfel A (2002) Gewalttätig durch Medien? Das Parlament. Aus Politik und Zeitgeschichte 44:29–37. http://www.bpb.de/files/P8CUER.pdf (Stand: 06/2009)

Lieberson S (1985) Making it count. The improvement of social research and theory. University of California Press, Berkeley

Mayer M (1992) Devianz im Kontext von Medienkonsum und Persönlichkeitsfaktoren. Unveröffentlichte Diplomarbeit, Regensburg

Merten K (1999) Gewalt durch Gewalt im Fernsehen? VS Verlag für Sozialwisseenschaften, Opladen

Paik H, Comstock G (1994) The effect of television violence on antisocial behavior: a meta-analysis. Commun Res 21:516–546

Raithel J (2003) Medien, Familie und Gewalt im Jugendalter. Zum Zusammenhang von Gewaltkriminalität, Erziehungserfahrungen, Filmkonsum und Computernutzung. Monatsschr Kriminol Strafrechtsreform 86:287–298

Scheungrab M (1993) Filmkonsum und Delinquenz. Ergebnisse einer Interviewstudie mit straffälligen und nicht-straffälligen Jugendlichen und jungen Erwachsenen. Roderer Verlag, Regensburg

Sherry JL (2001) The effect of violent video games on aggression. Hum Commun Res 27:409–431

Sutherland EA (1979) Die Theorie der differentiellen Kontakte. In: Sack F, König R (eds) Kriminalsoziologie, 3. Aufl. Akademische Verlagsgesellschaft, Wiesbaden, pp 395–399

Wild P (1992) Devianz im Kontext von Filmkonsum und anderen Freizeitaktivitäten. Unveröffentlichte Diplomarbeit, Regensburg

Internet Dependency: Symptoms, Diagnosis and Therapy

Bert Theodor teWildt

Abstract The question of whether people can become dependent on media in a pathological sense has come to the fore with the development of the internet and its derivatives. Apart from the fact that the mental development of an individual living in a civilisation necessarily takes place in dependency on its media and their mediation functions, there is increasing evidence that the realms of the media in cyberspace are taking on dynamics of their own to which people are becoming enslaved in the sense of an *addiction*. The convergence of all precursor analogue media in the digital world and the novel interactivity with which it is capable of connecting all contents and people may explain why using the internet can lead to dependency in a clinically relevant sense.

1 Latest Research on the Phenomenon of Internet Dependency

The phenomenon of internet dependency was first described by the New York psychiatrist Ivan Goldberg in 1995, initially meant ironically. As a reaction to the internet euphoria of his times, Goldberg drew up a symptom list for internet dependency, analogous to the criteria for dependency disorders of DSM-IV, and sent it to expert colleagues as an email circular (Eichenberg and Ott 1999). To his own surprise, Goldberg received numerous replies in all seriousness from people who were sure that they were suffering from such a mental disorder. When the New York Times picked up on this phenomenon in 1966, the subject finally took off. Computer games had been suspected of being addictive much earlier, although the first studies only demonstrated a low pathological addictive potential in this connection (Soper and Miller 1983; Shotton 1989). While Goldberg lost interest in

B.T. teWildt (✉)
Centre for Psychological Medicine, Hannover Medical School, Hannover, Germany
e-mail: tewildt.bert@mh-hannover.de

K. Cornelius and D. Hermann (eds.), *Virtual Worlds and Criminality*,
DOI 10.1007/978-3-642-20823-2_5,

the subject, the American Kimberley Young turned into a pioneer in the research field of internet dependency (Young 1996). She was the first researcher to investigate this phenomenon systematically and critically in various different studies. On the basis of the DSM-IV criteria for pathological gambling, she developed analogous criteria for identifying internet dependents, in order then to investigate them in relation to demographics, media usage behaviour, comorbidity and other variables, and to generate initial evidence on how such people can be treated. Right from the start, Young made it clear in her papers that the psychopathologies caused by excessive use of the internet manifest themselves in very different ways, i.e. that it is of importance whether somebody in cyberspace mainly plays computer games, buys products, or searches for pornographic material, to name but a few. In this sense, Young (1998b) distinguished five different forms of disorder that have addictive internet use behaviour in common:

1. Cybersex addiction.
2. Addiction to virtual communities/friendships in chats and internet forums.
3. Compulsive use of internet contents in online games, shops and activities.
4. Information overload in connection with the use of databases.
5. Computer addiction with regard to gaming and programming, independently of the internet.

A similar classification can be found in Davis (2002), while Petry (2003) simplifies it down to three subtypes, the excessive "gamers", "surfers" and "chatters". These apparently somewhat indiscriminate classifications make it clear how awkwardly research still confronts the phenomenology and nosology of internet and computer dependency. To this extent, the term "pathological internet use" initially used by Young (1997) appears to be more appropriate as the term for addiction, as it implies not only quantitative but also qualitative aspects of harmful internet use, quite apart from the fact that the reference disease in accordance with the valid classification systems (DSM-IV and ICD-10) for mental diseases is also called *pathological gambling* and not *gambling addiction* (Saß et al. 1998; Dilling et al. 2004).

The problem of terminological definition, and thus also of nosological classification, has continued to the present day, as shown by Table 1, in which the different terms for the phenomenon of internet and computer dependency can be seen in their chronological occurrence. Both initially in the English-speaking and later also in the German-speaking world, there are different positions in relation to the question of diagnostic classification, which are also reflected in the nomenclature.

When classifying the phenomenon, three main streams of thought can be identified. The most correct choice of terminology in terms of clinical psychiatry and psychology is *pathological internet use*, but few researchers decided to use this (Davis 2001; Kratzer 2006). Most often, conceptionalisation as an *addiction* stands behind the choice of terminology. The less common use of the term *dependency* can be understood as a compromise solution, which accommodates the framework of the established psychiatric classification systems in the sense of a classification to the non-substance-related dependencies, but also acknowledges the symptomatological similarity to the substance-related disorders. Like the present paper, the first

Table 1 Terms for dependent use behaviour in relation to the internet

Term	Author(s) and year of publication
Pathological internet use (PIU)/internet addiction	Young (1996)
Internet addiction	Zimmerl and Panosch (1998)
Virtual addiction	Greenfield (1999)
Internet dependency	Seemann et al. (2000)
Internet addiction	Hahn and Jerusalem (2001)
Pathological/problematic internet use (PIU)	Davis (2001)
Internet dependency	Lin and Tsai (2002)
Online addiction	Farke (2003)
Internet dependency	te Wildt (2004)
Internet dependency	Möller et al. (2005)
Computer addiction	Bergmann and Hüther (2006)
Computer addiction	Grüsser and Thalemann (2006)
Pathological internet use	Kratzer (2006)

German-speaking psychiatric textbook to include this clinical picture (Möller et al. 2005) uses the term *internet dependency*. This neutral term, which is more phenomenologically descriptive than diagnostically classifying, has ultimately been chosen within the context of the present paper because it is by no means clear whether this circumscribed phenomenon is an independent clinical picture at all, or whether it is a symptom or syndrome that occurs as part of known mental disorders. Some authors (Shaffer et al. 2000) continue to completely reject the clinical importance of the phenomenon internet dependency from a psychiatric viewpoint.

2 Symptoms and Diagnosis of Internet Dependency

Even if the phenomenological classification remains unclear, there appears to be broad agreement among the scientists involved in research to date that the criteria for non-substance-related dependency, which are in turn oriented along the criteria for substance-related dependency disorders, can also be applied to internet dependency.

On the basis of this notion, as early as 1996 Young developed criteria for *internet addiction* of which at least five must be fulfilled in order to render the diagnosis. The eight Young criteria were later slightly modified by Beard and Wolf (2001) to the extent that the first five criteria, which relate exclusively to the primary symptoms of excessive internet consumption, must all be fulfilled and additionally at least one of the last three criteria, which tend to describe secondary negative sequelae, for the diagnosis to be rendered (Table 2).

He justified this tightening of the criteria with the argument that the first five criteria are by all means compatible with a regulated daily routine and that only the last three criteria point to a pathological dimension. Later, Beard postulated that a clinical interview was necessary to enable the diagnosis of internet dependency, himself suggesting a detailed catalogue of questions, but this never really became

Table 2 Diagnostic criteria for pathological internet use/internet dependency by Young (1996), modified by Beard and Wolf (2001)

All of the following criteria (1–5) must be present:
1. Is preoccupied with the internet (think about previous online activity or anticipate next online session)
2. Needs to use the internet with increased amounts of time in order to achieve satisfaction
3. Has made unsuccessful efforts to control, cut back, or stop internet use
4. Is restless, moody, depressed, or irritable when attempting to cut down or stop internet use
5. Has stayed online longer than originally intended
At least one of the following criteria (6–8) must be present:
6. Has jeopardized or risked the loss of a significant relationship, job, educational or career opportunity because of the internet
7. Has lied to family members, therapist, or others to conceal the extent of involvement with the internet
8. Uses the internet as a way of escaping from problems or of relieving a dysphoric mood (e.g., feelings of helplessness, guilt, anxiety, depression)

established (Beard 2005). However, the eight criteria became accepted in clinical and research settings in modified and unmodified form, more so than the criteria of the American Psychological Association, whose list of ten items included virtually all eight of the Young criteria and additionally two further somewhat redundant criteria that ask very generally whether there are withdrawal symptoms and whether the internet activities are continued despite an awareness of the negative consequences (APA 1999).

In the German-speaking world, several detailed psychometric instruments have become established. Seemann et al. (2000), for example, developed a "Questionnaire on internet use", which was applied in several further studies (Kratzer 2006). The best validated and most used questionnaire is the Internet Addiction Scale (ISS) of Hahn and Jerusalem (2001). In addition, a psychological test instrument for the diagnosis of computer game dependency in children (Thalemann et al. 2004) was applied in a number of studies investigating excessive or addictive computer use (Grüsser et al. 2005).

However, in view of the fact that the diagnostic conception of internet and computer game dependency has not been sufficiently characterised either qualitatively in its psychiatric phenomenology or quantitatively in its clinical incidence, a careful and critical handling of these undoubtedly very helpful instruments has been necessary to date.

3 Epidemiology of Internet Dependency

Since the instruments for investigating internet dependency have not really been validated for this purpose to date, applying the respective cut-off values to reliably distinguish mentally ill internet dependents from healthy internet users in a clinical sense, particularly the epidemiological studies, which all used questionnaires of this kind to obtain their results, must be considered with a certain degree of caution. With regard to excessive computer game behaviour in children and adolescents, three German studies revealed a prevalence of 6% (Thalemann et al. 2004) and 9.3% (Mößle et al. 2007). A similar study from the UK determined prevalence rates for excessive online computer gaming of 9.1% in adolescents and 2.5% in adults (Griffiths et al. 2004). For adults, epidemiological figures are available particularly for internet dependency. An American study by Greenfield (1999) revealed "abusive" internet use behaviour in 6% of internet users. In an investigation of Taiwanese students, Lin and Tsai (2002) found a much higher rate (11.7%) of dependents. Cultural and technological differences between countries undoubtedly play a major role in the spread of internet dependency, whereby South Korea currently appears to be the worst affected country. The reason for this is that subsidised internet access was provided by the government to all its citizens as a matter of economic policy. However, the most research is also conducted in this country and an elaborate support system for internet dependents is offered (Ko et al. 2007). For Germany, a study by Hahn and Jerusalem (2001) using the Internet Addiction Scale (ISS) determined slightly lower dependency rates among internet users (3.2%), whereby it is noticeable that the rate among young male internet users is much higher by comparison. However, these figures must also be considered with caution, not only just because of the already described methodological problems and the very different populations, target variables and instruments, but also because the use of new electronic media has again changed markedly in the meantime. An even more ubiquitous presence of computers and internet, particularly in children's rooms today, has probably led to the problem becoming more acute. However, the figures available to date already demonstrate that excessive internet consumption quite definitely represents a society-wide problem that is taking on epidemic proportions.

4 Internet Dependency and Comorbidity

Similar to substance-related dependency disorders, it also makes sense to consider comorbid disorders occurring together with non-substance-related internet dependency from two angles. To begin with, it must be considered which mental disorders occur in combination with internet dependency on the basis of the studies conducted to date. Then, from the viewpoint of other already known media-associated disorders, it will be a question of which psychopathologies and mental disorders manifest themselves particularly often in abnormal media use.

The studies that have investigated internet dependents for comorbidity to date can only be compared to a limited degree as a result of their often very different methodologies, which is particularly due to the fact that there is a lack of clarity in the diagnosis of internet dependency and that it is often difficult to clearly demonstrate whether or not the subjects included in the respective studies have a clinically relevant disorder at all. Moreover, many of the studies work with psychometric self-rating scales, often also computerised or anonymous via the internet. Without a clinical examination in direct contact, however, it is not possible to render a reliable psychiatric diagnosis. To this extent, the study results obtained to date can only be seen as pointers towards possible comorbidities of internet dependency, whereby the incidence data must be viewed with particular caution.

In a study by Black et al. (1998) almost all of the 21 internet dependents investigated fulfilled the criteria of one or more mental disorders, whereby particularly personality disorders (52%), substance-related dependency disorders (38%), affective disorders (33%) and anxiety disorders (18%) were diagnosed. Shapira et al. (2000) demonstrated an axis-I disorder according to DSM-IV in all of their internet-dependent study participants, whereby affective disorders, major depression and bipolar disorders as well as anxiety disorders were most common. All of the internet dependents examined by Greenfield (1999) also showed the criteria for at least one acute mental disease, among them predominantly depressive disorders.

Precisely depressive syndromes thus appear to be closely associated with the development of internet dependency. This is also shown in an investigation by Orzack and Orzack (1999) and in further studies that see an association between the factor depressivity in the subclinical sphere and excessive internet use (Bai et al. 2001; Morgan and Cotten 2003). Caplan (2003) also demonstrated that the factors depressivity and loneliness are significant predictors of the preference for online social contacts, i.e. that depressed and reclusive people tend to seek contact in the internet, which may lead to the risk of developing dependency in relation to the virtual world and further social impoverishment in relation to the concrete real world. Thus, a depressive development in the narrower sense can be consummated and intensified in an anxious-depressive regression in cyberspace. However, there are some studies – although they tend to be sociopsychological rather than clinical – that place in doubt the connection between depressivity and internet dependency (McKenna and Bargh 2000; LaRose et al. 2003). The only longitudinal study on this subject to date (Kraut et al. 1998) initially showed a correlation between the extent of internet use and the degree of depressive characteristics. However, the catamnestic examination of the same subjects did not confirm this correlation, which suggests that adaptive effects may occur with respect to a more appropriate use of the internet as people mature with age. However, since this longitudinal study investigated subclinical factors and effects in healthy people, it contributes little about the comorbidity of internet dependency and depressive disorders. On the contrary, such longitudinal studies can help to expose the chronological and causal connections between the characteristics depressivity and internet dependency.

The studies conducted to date thus suggest that the majority of those people who can be identified as internet dependents with the means available to date indeed fulfil the criteria for a known mental disorder. Depressive disorders, anxiety disorders and personality disorders appear to be particularly prevalent in connection with internet dependency. A not inconsiderable number of researchers (e.g. Shaffer et al. 2000; Griffiths 2000; Greenfield 1999) come to the conclusion that internet dependency can be understood as a novel symptom of known mental disorders.

This might also apply to further mental disorders for which, conversely, a comorbid internet dependency was observed, for example dissociative disorders and attention deficit hyperactivity syndrome (ADHS). People with complex dissociative disorders appear to be at particular risk of shifting their symptoms to a virtual plane where they can emerge in an infinite number of different identities (Köhler and Frindte 2003; te Wildt et al. 2006). While excessive television consumption does not appear to be a predictor for the development of ADHS in childhood (Acevedo-Polakovich and Pugzles Lorch 2006; Stevens and Mulsow 2006), there are several studies that suggest a connection between ADHS and computer game dependency (Chan and Rabinowitz 2006) or internet dependency (Ha et al. 2006) in children and adolescents.

The deliberations above about which psychopathologies translate in what way to a virtual plane and thus take on particular (psycho)dynamics, creates the impression that it is precisely neurotic disorders that develop a particular affinity to the media world and use cyberspace as a space for expression and field of action. However, it cannot be ruled out that the internet intensifies subclinical phenomena in a negative sense and thus itself becomes effective as a novel psychopathogenic force, which might develop into a risk particularly in young people with depressive and aggressive mood tendencies and with accentuated personality structures. Apart from this, it is to be suspected that children and adolescents who mainly grow up in virtual worlds, but then do not arrive either privately or professionally in a concrete real world they find attractive, secondarily fall ill with depression and anxiety disorders. However, the question arises whether these young people suffer more from what they experience in the virtual world or from what they miss and miss out on in their childhood and youth at home, in a circle of friends or at school. The experience gained in the investigation and treatment of internet dependents within the context of a clinic for media-associated disorders at the Hannover Medical School suggest that those affected often suffer from early attachment disorders.

5 Own Studies on the Diagnostic Classification of the Phenomenon *Internet Dependency*

An investigation of our own on the phenomenological and diagnostic classification of internet dependency was composed of a main study and three additional studies. To begin with, 25 patients were investigated who presented at the clinic for media-associated disorders of the psychiatric outpatients department I at the Hannover Medical School with internet dependency and a clinically relevant degree of suffering. Within the context of a comprehensive examination, a psychiatric diagnosis was initially rendered, which was checked with the aid of the structured clinical interview according to DSM-IV (SKID $_{I}$) and modified as necessary. In addition, the subjects completed a range of psychometric test instruments that contained both specific psychiatric phenomena and general psychopathological variables. The main instruments were the Internet Addiction Scale (ISS) and the

German version of the Barrat Impulsiveness Scale (BIS), which was also used for calculating the sample size. In order to enable a comparison with substance-related dependency disorders, the same instruments were additionally used to clinically examine 25 alcoholic subjects. In addition, 25 patients with depressive disorders and 25 patients with ADHS were tested psychometrically for pathological patterns of media use. All four patient groups were compared with a group of healthy subjects matched in each case for age, sex and school education.

The internet dependent subjects investigated were predominantly male (76%), were on average 29.4 years old and, despite slightly above-average school qualifications, had comparatively rarely trained in a profession or had a job. They used the internet on average 6.5 h per day and spent most of their time there playing online games, especially role-playing in complex virtual parallel worlds. None of the internet and computer-game dependents exclusively played computer or console games that are not played with others via the internet. This suggests that precisely the relationship dimension introduced into the media world by the internet is responsible for the particular dependency potential. The internet dependents showed highly significantly higher results for the characteristics impulsiveness (BIS), depressivity (BDI) and ADHS symptoms (CAARS index), among others. In the examination and in the SKID-I, all 25 of the internet dependents investigated fulfilled the criteria for known mental disorders, which provided an explanation for the pathological media use behaviour as a complex symptom in the sense of failed neurotic conflict resolution. In this connection, particularly depressive disorders and, to a slightly lesser extent, anxiety disorders and personality disorders, especially narcissistic and emotionally unstable ones (cluster B) were diagnosed. Similar diagnoses were rendered for the alcoholics within the context of the same investigation paradigm, whereby the comorbidity rate was relatively low. Only 44% of the alcoholics fulfilled the criteria of another mental disorder. In the group of depressives, six subjects (24%) fulfilled the criteria for pathological internet use. These primarily depressive internet dependents showed strong similarities to those patients presenting primarily with an internet dependency with regard to socio-demographic characteristics. Pathological internet use was also found in six of the investigated ADHS patients (24%). And compared with the respective control groups, both the depressives and the ADHS patients had highly significantly higher results for internet dependency on the Internet Addiction Scale.

In contrast to alcohol dependency, which is recognised as an independent clinical picture, internet dependency appears rather to be a novel syndrome within the context of known mental disorders, even if there are phenomenological parallels to substance-related dependency and to the impulse-control disorders. Particularly affected are young men who, on their way from adolescence into self-determined adult life, fail at school, at work or in private life and, aggrieved, insecure and mostly depressive, withdraw into virtual parallel worlds where they can play the hero that they cannot be in the concrete real world. In the sense of a post-modern transformation of symptoms, it is to be expected that psychopathologies will in this way be displaced to a virtual plane and develop dynamics of their own, not only in depressive patients, anxiety patients and ADHS patients, but in principle among all people suffering from mental disorders.

6 Approaches to Explaining the Phenomenon of *Internet Dependency*

Phenomenologically, there is much to suggest that the new digital media, in light of their ubiquitous availability and their apparently limitless interactivity, create a dimension of relationship to their consumers that is novel to the media, which can promote the development of dependency (Heim 1998). Contact-providing communication systems enable the user to cross virtual boundaries, which was not possible or was taboo in real life up to now. The attraction of playing games with control and loss of control also suggests a dependency potential here. Finally, an intensified physiological appeal to the senses compared with the *old* new media and interactive participation via keyboard and joystick lead to an elevated overall physiological stimulation in which endogenous reward systems undoubtedly also play a role. This plays a particular role precisely in the developing brain. In order to better understand the peculiarities of internet dependency, possible explanations will be put forward below in terms of neurobiology, learning theory and depth psychology.

Analogously to dependence on addictive substances and gambling, the development of internet dependency can be described neurobiologically. Even if research results are not yet available on such connections, it can be said with considerable certainty that functional aspects of specific neuroanatomical structures play just as much a role as the related neurochemical transmitter systems. On the basis of known neurobiological correlates of dependency, Bergmann and Hüther (2006) developed a model to explain what they call *computer addiction*, whereby they too see a particular potential for dependency precisely in the interactivity of the internet. The reward system located somewhere in the diencephalon plays a particular role in their model, therein particularly the neurochemical mediation by dopamine and endogenous opiates. The endogenous opiates appear here as the true mediators of pleasurable sensation following reward and thus mark the positively experienced biochemical endpoint of all addictive behaviours. The release of dopamine, in contrast, not only seems to announce the outstanding and expected reward, but also acts as a neuroplastic messenger in order to channel and strengthen certain neuronal connections. In the case of internet dependency, the repetition of certain virtual experiences, which is accompanied by distinctly positive sensations (release of opiates), will thus lead via habituation and expectation (release of dopamine) to neuronally strengthened channelling of certain sensory, cognitive and behavioural patterns. This is an indication that approaches to explaining internet dependency based in learning theory and depth psychology are inseparable from neurobiological ones.

The neurobiological reward system can thus also be understood as a somatic correlate of conditioning processes, which on the part of learning theory provide an explanation for the development of addictive behaviours. A wide range of different stimuli and affects in the internet can function as positive amplifiers of internet dependency: Getting the highest score in a computer game, a group experience within the context of an internet role-play, finding the desired information using a search engine, establishing a friendship or an erotic virtual relationship are just a few examples of how the repetition of positively experienced affects can lead to an affinity to and even dependency on the medium that provides them (Grüsser and Thalemann 2006). The fact that these types of experience are sought after at all in a virtual setting can be explained from the viewpoint of learning theory by an inadequate stress and affect regulation in the concrete real world. Experiences of humiliation and loneliness, for example, function as negative amplifiers here. Compensation of negative feelings that arise in contact with the concrete real world with positively perceived virtual experiences can then lead to a vicious circle in the sense of an avoidance strategy that is predestined to fail. Negative amplification by the increase in concrete psychosocial isolation and impoverishment then makes a repetition of the pathological media use pattern increasingly probable, up to the development of dependency.

Approaches towards explaining internet dependency based on depth psychology set their sights earlier in developmental psychology. From this perspective, the even more fundamental question posed is what causes individuals to withdraw from the concrete real world and from relationships with other people, i.e. what comes before the avoidance behaviour. On the basis of the research findings to date that precisely depressive disorders and anxiety disorders – not uncommonly also against the backdrop of personality disorders – are diagnosed in patients with internet dependency, the phenomenon might be understood as the expression of an anxious-depressive regression. In this way, internet dependency might be explained as a symptom of a spectrum of known mental disorders. If, for example, a narcissistically aggrieved depressive plays the hero in an internet role-play, or an insecure sociophobe can only establish contacts to other people in chats, the symptom appears not only as an avoidance strategy but also as an attempt at conflict resolution, the failure of which accounts for the development of dependency. Here, it becomes clear that the approaches of depth psychology to explaining internet dependency are less concerned with the quantitative aspects of dependency than with the qualitative aspects of the mental disorders concealed behind it and the characteristically used media contents.

Neurobiological, learning theoretical and depth psychological approaches are by no means mutually exclusive, rather they complement each other. While neurobiological aspects represent the somatic correlates of mental processes, learning theory tends to describe the psychological functional level and depth psychology rather the level of psychological meaning.

7 Nosology of the Phenomenon *Internet Dependency*

From a psychiatric point of view, there are in principle three ways to diagnostically classify the clinical phenomenon of internet dependency. These three approaches, which attempt to explain internet dependency as an impulse-control disorder, as a non-substance-related dependency in the sense of an *addiction*, or as a symptom of known mental disorders, are dealt with consecutively in the following.

If one decided to diagnose internet dependency as an independent disease entity, it would be classified in accordance with the classification systems of DSM-IV (Saß et al. 1998) and ICD-10 (Dilling et al. 2004) as belonging to the impulse-control disorders. Apart from kleptomania, pyromania and trichotillomania, this includes pathological gambling, which can be considered to be a reference disorder. In the category "specified impulse-control disorder", internet dependency would accordingly be labelled as "pathological internet use". However, the entire disease category of impulse-control disorders appears to be a rather questionable construct for various reasons. Among other things, intrinsically pathological and criminal behaviours, such as stealing, playing with fire and tearing out hair, are thrown into one category with behaviours that are not pathological per se but occur in excessive form. If one takes a closer look, there is much to suggest that kleptomania, pyromania, trichotillomania and non-substance-related dependency are to be understood as symptoms of antecedent or deeper lying disorders. It would not be surprising whether, against the backdrop of these observations, the questionability of the construct of impulse-control disorders is recognised in the near future and taken into consideration in the new editions of the diagnostic classification systems. This would also be supported by the fact that, conversely, impulse-control disorders also occur in many other diseases (Grant et al. 2005), whereby they can manifest themselves in very many different types and ways, not just in the sense of the substance-related or non-substance-related dependency forms defined here. They include, for example compulsive diseases and mania on axis I of the DSM-IV and emotionally unstable personality disorder of the impulsive or borderline type on axis II. Precisely in the latter two personality disorders, impulsivity and substance abuse are characteristic signs of a primary disease that must not be overlooked as a result of symptomatic abuse and dependency phenomena being overrated. Here, the term *pathological internet use* would have the advantage that it would not only imply disorders in the quantitative sense, i.e. dependency on the internet, but also a pathological form of use in the qualitative sense, when not so much the duration as the content points to pathological use of the internet. However, to create the category *pathological media use* alongside *pathological gambling* within the context of the group of *impulse-control disorders* is controversial, even if this position is justified to the extent that an increasing number of people are undeniably presenting in psychiatric and psychotherapeutic clinics and practices primarily due to internet dependency. To this extent, the establishment of a classification for media dependency is also important with regard to the assumption of costs by the health insurance agencies and the necessary installation of specific outpatient and inpatient clinics in the healthcare system.

Supporters of the disease concept of the so-called *behavioural addictions* advocate the establishment of a new category, analogous to the substance-related dependency disorders, which should also be included in the psychiatric classification systems (Rosenthal 2003). The most comprehensive and convincing review on this subject is by Grüsser and Thalemann (2006). They prefer the addiction model to the concept of an impulse-control disorder, since it is clearly based on a previously existing disease concept which shows marked phenomenological similarities and thus also implies similar therapeutic consequences. The latter is remarkable to the extent that there are no uniform therapeutic approaches to cover the very heterogeneous group of impulse-control disorders. The term *behavioural addiction*, however, is problematic since the term addiction was completely removed from ICD-10 and DSM-IV some years ago in favour of the terms *abuse* and *dependency*. Having said that, there is much to suggest that behaviours can indeed cause addiction in a similar way to psychotropic substances. From the purely phenomenological standpoint, there are many areas in which the criteria for substance-related dependency can be seen to be applicable to the symptoms of internet dependency. For example, all of the subjects examined at the Hannover Medical School fulfilled the criteria formulated on the basis of substance-related dependencies and displayed a significant level of suffering. In order to distinguish more clearly from substance-related dependency, it is helpful to take a closer look at the respective substrate or psychotropic agent of the non-substance-related dependency disorders. If one excludes sport and sex as behaviours causing dependency, because neurotransmitters released by the specific activation of the reward system and other areas of the brain lead to a kind of *endogenous substance-related dependency*, that leaves gambling, work, shopping and media use. The fact that pathological gambling is the first and thus far only recognised non-substance-related dependency disorder is plausible because the substrate can be relatively clearly named here, even if there is a relatively high number of comorbidities, in particular narcissistic and depressive disorders (Petry and Jahreeiss 1999), through which pathological gambling can also be understood as a symptom. The substrate of *gambling dependency* is primarily the winning of money. In contrast to the other three suggested *behavioural addictions* (Grüsser and Thalemann 2006) which relate to more or less complex behaviours and in which a large number of stimuli lead to the addictive effect, in pathological gambling it is a question of winning money, a risky reward but one that increases the feeling of self-esteem and just requires the taking of risk and of course the staking of money. The fact that the relatively simple stimulus-reaction pattern, which only knows the dopamine-mediated tense expectation and is resolved either in winning or in losing, leads to a conditioning that demonstrably shows clear and characteristic neurobiological correlates (Bechara 2003), places this disorder closer to the substance-related dependency disorders, even if a gambling-dependent person does not have to gamble as frequently as a substance-dependent person has to consume addictive substances in order not to experience withdrawal. Until a differentiation between substance-related and non-substance-related dependency down to the neurobiological level is possible, on the basis of a phenomenological consideration of the dependency substrates one could speak of a continuum between substance-related dependency (addiction) and non-substance-related dependency (impulse control). Whereas substance dependency has a clear physical substrate in the addictive substance, impulse-control disorders relating to the body in connection with sex and sport tend to be mediated by endogenous neurophysiological substrates. Non-substance-related dependencies not relating to the body with simple stimulus-reaction patterns, such as pathological gambling, in which the neurobiological dependency dimension is relatively well documented, can be understood as a link to the dependency of more complex behaviours, such as internet use. An intermediate position between pathological gambling and pathological internet use may be taken up by the dependency of first-person shooters, in whom the substrate or the stimulus leading to the release of adrenalin is the killing of a virtual enemy and the accompanying points won. However, the playing of internet role-play games, in which most internet dependents partake, is far too complex for a clear addictive agent to be identified. In these games, the internet users are exposed to very different stimuli and are looking for very different types of experience. It is by no means just a question of living out aggression, action and thrills, but friendship, romance and sexuality. Such internet users are thus dependent on a whole parallel world, which they generally consider to be more attractive than the concrete world of their real life. To ignore these qualitative content-related aspects of feeling, thinking and acting and reduce it to a dependency on the medium itself as an *addictive phenomenon* to be understood purely quantitatively would undoubtedly do no justice to the persons affected either in their external or internal world.

In light of the study result obtained to date, there is much to suggest that a known mental disorder is always concealed behind the phenomenon of internet dependency. Similar to the study by Kratzer (2006), all of the internet dependents examined at the Hannover Medical School fulfilled the criteria for another mental disorder, whereby the study in question particularly yielded evidence of a connection with depressive disorders, to a lesser degree also with anxiety and personality disorders as well as ADHS. Even if the results of the studies conducted to date suggest that a mentally healthy adult will not become dependent on the internet and its derivatives *de novo*, it is not possible to give the all-clear in this sense. In view of the suggestive and interactive power of the new digital media, in particular that of online games and parallel worlds, it cannot be excluded that people with subclinical psychiatric syndromes, but particularly also children and adolescents, may become dependent and suffer mental disease. In this way, three scenarios in which internet and computer game dependency might develop into a primary clinical picture are conceivable.

The first reason lies in the fact that the media world in cyberspace appears to be developing dynamics of its own that are capable of taking hold of and captivating the individual as no medium has done before. The results of the latest investigations suggest that online role-play games have the greatest potential for dependency. The reason for this is that the game developers make sure that they establish an intensive bond with their users, sometimes using perfidious methods to draw them into a widely woven web of relationships with other users. Apart from this, they offer their users an alternative living environment in which they can apparently be and do things that are not possible in the concrete real world. At all times being able to disappear into a fantasy world and constantly assume a different identity and start new relationships, that is what makes for the particular temptation of the digital parallel universes. Falling into their trap, becoming dependent on them, is not just the fate of people with antecedent mental disorders, even if the studies conducted to date might suggest this. If one looks at the development in South Korea, that country which was first to establish a comprehensive, state-funded supply of internet connections, an almost epidemic spread of internet and computer game dependency can be seen there (Hur 2006), which is difficult to explain in terms of a symptom transformation of known mental disorders alone. The fact that numerous different treatment options are now available for internet dependents there, in some cases in special clinics specifically instituted for this purpose, and that research on this subject is the most advanced in international comparison, may be taken as an indication that we are not just concerned with a sociological problem here but undoubtedly with an epidemiologically relevant disease phenomenon. In the meantime, similar developments can also be observed in Taiwan (Yen et al. 2008; Ko et al. 2008) and in China (Huang et al. 2007; Cao et al. 2007). For a country such as Germany, this may mean that the internet dependents who have become clinically conspicuous to date are merely the tip of the iceberg, which in our present study is revealed by the fact that the subjects examined show a particularly pronounced psychopathology.

Second, in the subclinical sense, people affected by mental disorders who perhaps have never needed psychiatric treatment may as a result of dependent media use decompensate mentally for the first time and become manifestly ill (Ratey and Johnson 1998). This logical supposition implies that the attempt to categorise internet dependency either as a symptom *or* as the catalyst of a disease falls short of the mark. In the vast majority of mental diseases, a multifactorial genesis is assumed. Careful research and treatment of these disorders requires a comprehensive consideration of all factors. At the latest with the rapid growth of the internet, there is now a need to consider excessive media use in quantitative and qualitative terms as a risk factor for the development of mental diseases.

This applies, third, especially to children and adolescents, whose mental and emotional development is particularly susceptible to damaging influences. Even if it should turn out that a mentally healthy adult is in little danger of becoming trapped in a clinically relevant dependency on the internet and its derivatives, this cannot be simply transferred to children and adolescents. Alongside committed psychiatry for adults, adolescents and children, education in all aspects of the media is necessary, not just in the mediation of so-called *media competence* but also including concepts for a prevention of internet and computer game dependency. These deliberations make it clear just how much the phenomenon of internet dependency necessitates a collaboration of different media-scientific disciplines.

8 Therapy and Prevention of Internet Dependency

Since the approaches presented above for explaining and classifying internet dependency are still a relatively long way away from being scientifically founded, no evidence-based therapy recommendations can be given at present. The therapeutic approaches taken to date can be roughly classified according to the major psychotherapy orientations. Behavioural therapy, based on learning therapy, which classifies internet dependency as an addictive disease, recommends those behavioural therapy measures that have proved successful in the treatment of people with substance-related dependencies. And the depth psychological therapy procedures based on psychoanalytical findings, which tend to understand non-substance-related dependency phenomena as symptoms of known mental disorders, recommend the psychotherapeutic treatment of precisely these primary diseases. If the antecedent or comorbid mental disorders are accompanied by a correspondingly high degree of suffering, somatic therapeutic approaches may additionally be indicated, especially the administration of psychotropic drugs. In the following, the suggestions for treating internet dependency put forward to date are presented briefly in accordance with the explanatory approaches described above.

Neurobiological therapeutic approaches, as already indicated, may be based on a treatment of the antecedent or comorbid mental disorder with psychotropic drugs. As it is predominantly a question of depressions and anxiety syndromes here, a particular role is played by sedatives in the acute phase and antidepressants in long-term treatment. However, there is evidence that antidepressants generally have positive effects in the treatment of dependency disorders, regardless of the occurrence of a depressive syndrome in the narrower sense. Substances that are supposed to explicitly reduce craving in dependency disorders have already been applied with a certain amount of success to maintain abstinence in pathological gamblers and other non-substance-related dependency disorders. However, such opiate antagonists will probably not have a place in the treatment of internet dependency, for the one reason alone that absolute abstinence is in general unlikely to be the goal of therapy.

Cognitive behavioural therapeutic approaches, which are oriented along the treatment of substance-related dependencies, are the therapeutic procedures recommended by far the most commonly in the literature for treating internet dependency. This applies not only to the initially leading researchers from the Anglo-American world (Young 1999; Greenfield 1999), but also to German researchers, in particular the research group led by Grüsser and Wölfling (Grüsser and Thalemann 2006). The cognitive therapy component is aimed at the analysis and modification of pathological cognitive processes with regard to the identification of positive amplifiers (virtual rewards) and negative amplifiers (real humiliation). The behavioural therapy component is aimed more at the concrete modification of behavioural patterns, whereby it is mainly a question of replacing the pathological media use behaviour with positive experience and behaviour patterns in the concrete real world.

Psychodynamic approaches first attempt to determine what it is in the concrete real world that is so offensive or morbid and what it is in the virtual world that is experienced as being so positive and is sought after (te Wildt 2004). These questions already play a decisive role for the diagnosis of the deeper lying disorders. By uncovering the underlying psychodynamics that describe the movement from the real into the virtual world, it is possible to find distance to it. The experience of the relationship with the psychotherapist plays a particular role here, as it takes place in the concrete real world. Within the context of this relationship, new experiences and affects can be opened up and made experienceable, which can ultimately be transferred to the client's real-life environment.

Which psychotherapeutic procedures will prove to be helpful in the treatment of internet dependency in the long term can only be determined once the clinical picture itself has been better researched in its basic characteristics; both of the main psychotherapeutic procedures will probably prove to be beneficial in different patients and in different phases of the disease.

References

Acevedo-Polakovich ID, Pugzles Lorch E (2006) Disentangling the relation between television viewing and cognitive process in children with attention-deficit/hyperactivity disorder and comparison children. Arch Pediatr Adolesc Med 160:354–360

American Psychological Association (APA) (1999) Ten criteria for internet addiction (online publication). http://www.apa.org/releases/internet.html

Bai YM, Lin CC, Chen JY (2001) Internet addiction disorder among clients of a virtual clinic. Psychiatr Serv 52:1394–1397

Beard KW (2005) Internet addiction: a review of current assessment techniques and potential assessment questions. Cyberpsychol Behav 1:7–14

Beard KW, Wolf EM (2001) Modification in the proposed diagnostic criteria for internet addiction. Cyberpsychol Behav 4:377–383

Bechara A (2003) Risky business: emotion, decision-making and addiction. J Gambl Stud 19:23–51

Bergmann W, Hüther G (2006) Computersüchtig. Kinder im Sog der Medien. Walter, Düsseldorf

Black DW, Repertinger S, Gaffney GR, Gaebel J (1998) Family history and psychiatric comorbidity in persons with compulsive buying: preliminary findings. Am J Psychiatry 155:960–963

Cao F, Su L, Liu T, Gao X (2007) The relationship between impulsivity and internet addiction in a sample of Chinese adolescents. Eur Psychiatry 22:466–471

Caplan SE (2003) Preference for online social interaction: a theory of problematic internet use and psychosocial well-being. Commun Res:625–648

Chan PA, Rabinowitz T (2006) A cross-sectional analysis of video games and attention deficit hyperactivity disorder symptoms in adolescents. Ann Gen Psychiatry 5:1–16

Davis RA (2001) A cognitive-behavioral model of pathological internet use (PIU). Comput Hum Behav 17:187–195

Davis RA (2002) Validation of a new scale for measuring problematic internet use. Implications for pre-employment screening. Cyberpsychol Behav 5:331–345

Dilling H, Mombour W, Schmidt MH (2004) Internationale Klassifikation psychischer Störungen. ICD-10 Kapitel V (F), Weltgesundheitsorganisation (WHO). Huber, Berne

Eichenberg C, Ott R (1999) Suchtmaschine Internetabhängigkeit: Massenphänomen oder Erfindung der Medien? c´t 19:106

Farke G (2003) Onlinesucht. Wenn Mailen und Chatten zum Zwang werden. Kreuz-Verlag, Stuttgart

Grant JE, Levine L, Kim D, Potenza MN (2005) Impulse control disorders in adult psychiatric inpatients. Am J Psychiatry 162:2184–2188

Greenfield DN (1999) Virtual addiction. New Harbinger, Oakland

Griffiths M (2000) Does internet and computer "addiction" exist? Some case study evidence. Cyberpsychol Behav 2:211–218

Griffiths MD, Davies MNO, Chappell D (2004) Online computer gaming. A comparison of adolescent and adult gamers. J Adolesc 27:87–96

Grüsser SM, Thalemann R (2006) Computersüchtig? Rat und Hilfe. Huber, Berne

Grüsser SM, Thalemann R, Albrecht U (2005) Exzessive Computernutzung im Kindesalter – Ergebnisse einer psychometrischen Erhebung. Wien Klin Wochenschr 117:188–195

Ha JH, Yoo HJ, Cho IH, Chin B, Shin D, Kim JH (2006) Psychiatric comorbidity assessed in Korean children and adolescents who screen positive for internet addiction. J Clin Psychiatry 67:821–826

Hahn A, Jerusalem M (2001) Internetsucht: Jugendliche gefangen im Netz. In: Raithel J (ed) Risikoverhalten Jugendlicher. Leske & Budrich, Opladen

Heim M (1998) Virtual realism. Oxford University Press, New York

Huang Z, Wang M, Qian M, Zhong J, Tao R (2007) Chinese internet addiction inventory: developing a measure of problematic internet use for Chinese college students. Cyberpsychol Behav 10:805–811

Hur MH (2006) Demographic, habitual, and socioeconomic determinants of internet addiction disorder: an empirical study of Korean teenagers. Cyberpsychol Behav 9:514–525

Ko CH, Yen JY, Yen CF, Lin HC, Yang MJ (2007) Factors predictive for incidence and remission of internet addiction in young adolescents: a prospective study. Cyberpsychol Behav 10:545–551

Ko CH, Yen JY, Chen CS, Chen CC, Yen CF (2008) Psychiatric comorbidity of internet addiction in college students: an interview study. CNS Spectr 13:147–153

Köhler T, Frindte W (2003) Internetnutzung und multiple personality disorder. In: Ott R, Eichenberg C (eds) Klinische psychologie und internet, vol 6. Hogrefe, Göttingen

Kratzer S (2006) Pathologische Internetnutzung. Eine Pilotstudie zum Störungsbild. Pabst, Lengerich

Kraut R, Patterson M, Lundmark V, Kiesler S, Mukopadhyay T, Scherlis W (1998) Internet paradox. A social technology that reduces social involvement and psychosocial well-being? Am Psychol 53:1017–1031

LaRose R, Eastin M, Gregg J (2003) Reformulating the internet paradox: Social cognitive explanations of internet use and depression. J Online Behav. http://www.behavior.net/JOB/v1n2/paradox.html, accessed on 2.7.2011

Lin SS, Tsai CC (2002) Sensation seeking and internet dependence of Taiwanese high school adolescents. Comput Hum Behav 18:411–426

McKenna K, Bargh J (2000) Plan 9 from cyberspace: the implications of the internet for personality and social psychology. Pers Soc Psychol Rev 4:57–75

Möller HJ, Laux G, Deister A (2005) Psychiatrie und Psychotherapie. Thieme, Stuttgart

Morgan C, Cotten S (2003) The relationship between internet activities and depressive symptoms in a sample of college freshmen. Cyberpsychol Behav 6:133–142

Mößle T, Kleimann M, Rehbein F (2007) Bildschirmmedien im Alltag von Kindern und Jugendlichen. Problematische Mediennutzungsmuster und ihr Zusammenhang mit Schulleistungen und Aggressivität. Nomos, Baden-Baden

Orzack M, Orzack D (1999) Treatment of computer addicts with complex co-morbid psychiatric disorders. Cyberpsychol Behav 2:465–473

Petry J (2003) Pathologischer PC-Gebrauch: Nosologische Einordnung und Falldarstellungen. In: Ott R, Eichenberg C (eds) Klinische Psychologie und Internet. Potenziale für klinische Praxis, Intervention, Psychotherapie und Forschung. Hogrefe, Göttingen, pp 257–70

Petry J, Jahreeiss R (1999) Stationäre medizinische Rehabilitation von "Pathologischen Glücksspielern": Differentialdiagnostik und Behandlungsindikation. Dtsch Rentenversicherung 4:196–218

Ratey JJ, Johnson C (1998) Shadow syndromes: the mild forms of major mental disorders that sabotage US. Bantam Doubleday Dell, New York

Rosenthal RJ (2003) Distribution of the DSM-IV criteria for pathological gambling. Commentaries. Addiction 98:1674–1675

Saß H, Wittchen HU, Zaudig M (1998) Diagnostisches und Statistisches Manual Psychischer Störungen, DSM-IV, 2nd edn. Hogrefe, Göttingen

Seemann O, Stefanek J, Quadflieg N, Grebener S, Kratzer S, Möller-Lehmkühler AM, Ziegler W, Engel RR, Hegerl U (2000) Wissenschaftliche Online-Umfrage zur Internetabhängigkeit. Forschritte Med 118:109–113

Shaffer HJ, Hall MN, Vander-Bilt J (2000) "Computer addiction": a critical consideration. Am J Orthopsychiatry 70:162–168

Shapira N, Goldsmith T, Keck P Jr, Khosla U, McElroy S (2000) Psychiatric features of individuals with problematic internet use. J Affect Disord 57:267–272

Shotton M (1989) Computer Addiction? A study of computer dependency. Taylor & Francis, London

Soper WB, Miller MJ (1983) Junk time junkies: an emerging addiction among students. Sch Couns 31:40–43

Stevens T, Mulsow T (2006) There is no meaningful relationship between television exposure and symptoms of attention-deficit/hyperactivity disorder. Pediatrics 117:665–672

te Wildt BT (2004) Psychische Wirkungen der neuen digitalen Medien. Fortschr Neurol Psychiatr 72:574–585

te Wildt BT, Kowalewski E, Meibeyer F, Huber T (2006) Identität und Dissoziation im Cyberspace: Kasuistik einer dissoziativen Identitätsstörung im Zusammenhang mit einem Internet-Rollenspiel. Nervenarzt 77:81–84

Thalemann R, Alebrecht U, Thalemann C, Grüsser SM (2004) Kurzbeschreibung und psychometrische Kennwerte des "Fragebogens zum Computerspielverhalten bei Kindern" (CSVK). Psychomed 16:116–133

Yen JY, Ko CH, Yen CF, Chen SH, Chung WL, Chen CC (2008) Psychiatric symptoms in adolescents with internet addiction: comparison with substance use. Psychiatry Clin Neurosci 62:9–16

Young KS (1996) Internet addiction: the emerge of a new clinical disorder. Cyberpsychol Behav 1:237–244

Young KS (1997) What makes the internet addictive: potential explanations for pathological internet use. Paper presented at the 105th annual conference of the American Psychological Association, August 15, 1997, Chicago

Young KS (1998a) Caught in the net. Wiley, New York

Young KS (1998b) Internet addiction: symptoms, evaluation, and treatment. In: Vandecreek L, Jackson TL (eds) Innovations in clinical practice, vol 17. Professional Resource Press, Sarasota, pp 19–31

Zimmerl HD, Panosch B (1998) "Internetsucht" – Eine neumodische Krankheit? Wien Z Suchtforschung 4:19–34

Conflict Resolution in Virtual Worlds: General Characteristics and the 2009 Dutch Convictions on Virtual Theft

Arno R. Lodder

Abstract Conflicts are inherent to any society and do also occur in virtual worlds. As with normal conflicts, you can just leave them, or you could even leave the specific virtual world. However, when there is money involved, or participants have other than monetary interests, they may want to resolve their conflicts. Basically, there are three options. Players can try to resolve their conflicts themselves, they can ask the producer of the world to intervene, or they can ask governments for help. In my presentation, I will discuss the different norm levels applicable in virtual worlds (between players, from the producer, from the government), and illustrate the working of the different levels by elaborating upon several legal cases.

1 Introduction

If conflicts arise online, a natural environment to resolve these conflicts is the internet. It depends of course on the nature of the conflict, but for example all online trade conflicts can be resolved by what is generally referred to as Online Dispute Resolution (ODR). This is nicely illustrated by the dispute resolution services offered by eBay/Paypal through which more than 50 million conflicts on a yearly basis are resolved. In 90% of the cases, the disputing parties resolve the conflict through online negotiation, without any human intervention being necessary.

Virtual worlds are graphical, three-dimensional environments on the internet. It therefore makes sense to consider ODR services (hence: dispute resolution services offered over the internet) for the resolution of conflicts between users of virtual worlds. Ideally, the resolution of virtual conflicts should take place within the virtual world where it has arisen. The following picture illustrates how the internet

A.R. Lodder (✉)
Department Transnational Legal Studies, Computer/Law Institute, Vrije Universiteit Amsterdam, Amsterdam, The Netherlands
e-mail: a.r.lodder@vu.nl

K. Cornelius and D. Hermann (eds.), *Virtual Worlds and Criminality*,
DOI 10.1007/978-3-642-20823-2_6, © Springer-Verlag Berlin Heidelberg 2011

builds on and is part of the physical world, and virtual worlds on their turn build on and are part of the internet.

It is certainly not true for all cases, but for many cases one can argue that resolution of online conflicts in the physical world is a step back. A similar argument applies to virtual world conflicts that are resolved with existing ODR services. In a similar vein, one could argue that online resolution of offline conflicts is an improvement over offline resolution for reasons such as speed, costs, convenience (see e.g. Katsh and Rifkin 2001; Lodder and Zeleznikow 2010). In our digitized society, many conflicts with an offline origin can be resolved online. A good example is the Cybersettle service.[1] A blind bidding system can be used by parties that only disagree about the amount of money to be paid. For instance, a dispute between two insurance companies about the amount to be paid by one of the parties if there is no discussion about liability. More than 180,000 disputes have been settled by the Cybersettle service since 2000, almost all of them had an offline origin.

In the last couple of years, several virtual world conflicts went to court, so the dispute was taken from the virtual world into the physical world. The opposite is also possible, virtual worlds can be used for the resolution of real-world conflicts. A very complicated conflict is the ongoing battle between Israeli and Palestinians. As one observant correctly mentioned, it does not matter who started first, we need to work towards solutions. Virtual worlds can be welcome platforms in this respect. Although there was some protest and disruption during negotiations on this topic in Second Life, at least no one will be physically harmed (See 'Gaza protest in SL - conflict resolution in virtual worlds?' (youtube) and 'Rita J. King on Non-Violence in Virtual Worlds' (youtube)).

This chapter does not cover how to design and use virtual worlds as a platform to resolve conflicts (see Lodder 2007). The focus is on virtual conflicts, so conflicts with an origin in the virtual world. First some general characteristics of virtual conflicts are discussed, and in what way these might influence the suitability of particular dispute resolution methods. After this general part, a type of conflict that is really interesting in the context of *Virtual worlds and Criminality* is discussed: Dutch court cases (Habbo and Runescape) from 2009 on virtual theft are discussed. In the case of the Habbo Hotel online actions and the transfer of virtual objects is qualified as theft. In the Runescape case misbehaviour in the physical world led to

[1] http://www.cybersettle.com.

the transfer of virtual objects, and also here the judge qualified the eventual transfer of virtual objects as theft. These cases nicely illustrate that virtual disputes are taken seriously by the judiciary.

2 General Characteristics: Three Levels of Norms

The Magic Circle is a metaphor for the border existing between the game environment and that what takes place outside the game:

> a game-design term that is used to describe the "line" that protects games from intersecting with the real world so much that the real world distracts from the experience (taken from Duranske 2007a).

The term is often used in the context of virtual worlds (see in particular Fairfield 2009), but was introduced by the Dutch scholar Huizinga in his *Homo Ludens*. In terms of conflict resolution, the Magic Circle suggests to resolve all game-related conflicts within the game itself, so within the virtual world. Once the border between what is inside a virtual world and what is outside the virtual world is crossed, the virtual world loses some of its magic. This is what the Magic Circle aims to prevent. This line of thought resembles the idea that the internet has a legal order of its own, and that government should not interfere with what takes place online. Until the mid-1990s, a group of internet entrepreneurs[2] defended this view, but over time this approach appeared to be not realistic, in particular not because of the enormous growth of the internet population. Interestingly enough, the enormous growth of virtual worlds could have an opposite effect, so maintaining the Magic Circle may be considered more important. With so many people involved, from so many different countries, it does not make much sense to resolve conflicts with traditional mechanisms.

In particular, intellectual property rights are enforced outside the game environment, even if the conflict is on virtual objects that do not exist outside the virtual world.[3] Also, offensive behaviour and discriminatory speech within virtual worlds is something that is normally not tolerated, neither is money laundering, recruiting terrorists and child pornography. All these examples are actually normal world activities that are transferred to the virtual world, so breaking the Magic Circle in these cases seems justifiable. As far as pure in-world behaviour is concerned, it normally is not necessary to step outside the virtual world. But these two, the virtual and 'normal' world coincide more and more. For example trading in virtual items can be purely in-world as such, but often real money is involved so players may want to have a course of action outside the game if contracts are not performed properly.

So sometimes the border of the Magic Circle can and should be crossed. The more severe and out of the context the actions in the virtual world are, the more

[2] Most notably John Perry Barlow, David Johnson and David Post.

[3] For instance, the case on virtual beds (Reuters 2007a).

likely it is that one falls back to traditional law. Under these circumstance alternative dispute resolution, as it is based on cooperation and voluntariness, does not work, so only litigation then remains. In general, virtual conflicts can be resolved in variety of ways. First, by direct negotiation between the avatars having a conflict. If a conflict exists between two avatars about something that happened in-world, this is the preferred method. A good alternative might be to resolve conflicts using ODR services. A consequence is that the avatars should reveal their identity, although ODR service providers may accept parties to use avatar identities. Litigation concerning a pure virtual conflict does not seem to make much sense. There should at least be some link with the 'real' world such as money.

The important Dutch case law on virtual theft is discussed in length in the next section, but first some general characteristics are addressed that can help in deciding what way conflicts should be resolved. The discussion is shaped around the different levels of norms that play a role in regulating the behaviour of the avatars in virtual worlds. Basically, norms applicable to virtual worlds exist on three levels[4]:

Rules of the game, terms of service
Social norms
Legal norms

2.1 Rules of the Game, Terms of Service

Anyone entering a virtual world can do so only after signing a license agreement. This contract lays down the basic rules applying to the users of the virtual world. In the virtual world players interact, and the first set of rules applying to this interaction comes from the license agreement. So, on this first level the norms are based upon the relation between the producer of the game, and each single user. Just as people entering a shop have to obey the norms of the shop owner, or as the visitors of a dance party should follow what the organiser imposes. A difference is that a virtual world is partly or largely, depending on the nature of the virtual world, the result of the player's actions. Anyway, the interaction of the players, and their creations, are in the first place governed by a contract that indirectly applies to the relation between the players, namely via the producer. Therefore, the first level can be characterized as a vertical relation, but its impact is primarily horizontal.

Conflicts that originate in relation to these norms can be dealt with in different ways. In case the producer has a conflict with one of its users, he can enforce any sanction he considers appropriate. Since the producer normally is not active as an

[4]This distinction is the red line in the discussion of a series of virtual world cases in the book (in Dutch by Lodder and van Kokswijk 2008). This book elaborates on a research conducted for Rathenau.

avatar, the dispute resolution process cannot take place in the virtual world. In fact, if a player disagrees with what he is accused of, or with the sanction, he normally cannot do much against it. Virtual worlds do not have complaint mechanisms or other means to resolve these kinds of conflicts. If the conflict is serious enough, a player can go to court.[5]

Although the norms do not affect the relationship between players directly, occasionally players may want to sanction other players for not following the rules.[6] These kinds of conflicts can best be resolved in-world, by addressing the other player directly. Alternatively, players can complain to the producer, and hope an appropriate reaction will follow. If both former steps do not work, as a last resort the conflict can be taken outside the virtual world and taken to court.

2.2 *Social Norms*

At the second level norms are created by participants of the virtual world, mainly social norms. This second level norms regulate horizontally. Social norms can be simple rules of behaviour. For instance, that you should not disturb other players could be a social norm that players of a virtual world follow. Or that the leader of a guild decides what to do during an attack of another guild. If a member of a World of Warcraft guild does not appear in time on the appointment this member could get a warning or maybe even be excluded from the guild. Conflicts on this type of social norms are primarily handled in-world. As Linden Lab's general Counsel Martin Roberts puts it:

> Residents who find themselves in a disagreement with another resident are encouraged to resolve it directly as they would in any other context - online or offline (Kirby 2009).

Occasionally, those norms may overlap with the norms of the producer. Even if this is not the case the players may seek help from the producer. However, normally the producer will not step in, since it would mean that he chooses one player over the other.

In sophisticated virtual worlds, players can also define rules that apply to their territory, e.g. in Second Life. One might only allow people dressed in black, or people undressed. The sanctions of violating these norms are simple, you are expelled from the specific territory. Obviously, one might get a warning first, or might be allowed to return once the specific conditions are fulfilled. The conflicts on social norms related to a specific territory or specific guild are typically in-world conflicts that will be dealt with inside the virtual world. For instance, a virtual

[5]This is what happened in the Bragg case (see Reuters 2007b).

[6]For instance, in law suits against gold diggers, Hernandez v. Internet Gaming, Entertainment, Ltd et al. http://news.justia.com/cases/featured/florida/flsdce/1:2007cv21403/296927/.

mosque was visited by fascists (Julaybib 2007, http://archive.eteraz.org/story/2007/1/23/22353/3548). The owner of the mosque asked the members of the Front National to leave the mosque, and also filed a complaint at Linden Labs. Both did not have the desired effect, so the fascists were simply put on a black list and were no longer allowed to the mosque.

> The next day, on Muslim New Year, the mosque suffered multiple attacks, the first by two unknown avatars spouting anti-Semitic slogans and sitting on the Qur'an. An illegal script was then set off, which caused everyone inside the mosque to crash out of Second Life (Kuznicki 2007).

Since the electronic exclusion did not work, white listing was chosen as the way to regulate access to the virtual mosque. So from that moment on the mosque could only be entered by a closed user group.

2.3 Legal Rules

It depends on the nature of the virtual world what role the law can or should play. For instance, if the aim of the game is to insult people, you obviously cannot do anything about avatars calling you names. Or, if robbing and stealing is part of the game, you cannot complain about losing your property. One could argue that there should be a border between game purposes that are legal and those that no longer are. This is, however, a very delicate line. Should we allow a game which purpose is to abuse children? Or, a game which purpose is to kill people of a certain race? [7] This is a complicated debate that touches on the freedom of expression (freedom of thought), and falls beyond the scope of this paper. Conflicts on this level are primarily approached through state intervention,[8] although interest groups might take action as well.

Virtual worlds also differ on the freedom the players have to act, e.g. to create. If players cannot create, intellectual property issues are not that likely to occur. The more freedom players have to create, the more likely it is that players consider what has been created their intellectual property, and others may consider the creation an infringement on either a real world right or a virtual world right. If a real world right, e.g. a trade mark, is used without permission, the first reaction should be to ask the avatar to stop. Only if that does not work, it becomes sensible to start a court action. Alternative dispute resolution is not working under these circumstances, since apparently the avatar does not want to stop his illegal activities.

---

[7]E.g. Mark Wallace: "Imagine a game in which you have the choice of playing as a German WW2-era concentration camp administrator and your goal is to gather and kill as many Jews as possible", (in reply to Castronova 2005, TerraNova blog).

[8]Grand theft auto has been controversial, and some years ago British government as well as some other countries did forbid the game Man Hunt 2 in 2007 [Chris Borowski wrote a very good master thesis on this topic, in Dutch. See also Lodder (2008a)].

In general, avatars can resolve conflicts amicably. If this is not the case, the dispute will be between normal persons (behind the avatar). Difficult issues are then where to bring the summons, how to enforce the verdict, as it is legally not possible yet to use an avatar in court. So, a complication with starting a real-world action is that the real identity of the avatar has to be known, which normally is not easy to trace.[9]

Violation of contract can happen in virtual worlds. The normative framework for evaluating the contractual performance will be basically derived from real-world law. Just as is the case in the normal world, the value of the transaction normally will be too low to start a court action. ODR could help, in particular if it would be within the virtual world. Again, also here the first step to be taken is direct negotiation with the avatar that mal performed.

Contract law and intellectual property law, in particular copyright law, are the most relevant legal rules for virtual worlds. As Ross A. Dannenberg, partner at Banner and Witcoff, who represented a couple that claimed ownership of a virtual location known as Sailor's Cove states:

> while Second Life may be a virtual world, the intellectual property is real, the contracts are real, and residents are still subject to real world laws (Banner and Wittcoff 2008, http://www.bannerwitcoff.com/press/76/).

Other areas of law will be less often applicable. Privacy law is in relation to avatars a bridge too far, except if for instance the producer is misusing the personal information of its players. The continuous sending of messages in World of Warcraft by golddiggers offering all kinds of armoury, gold, etc. might be qualified as spam under anti-spam regulation, but a first complication already is that the sender normally would not fall under the jurisdiction of the European Union.

As already indicated, the state becomes interested if virtual world activities include discriminatory speech, money laundering, recruiting terrorists or child pornography. Although penal law may seem at first sight furthest away of legal norms to apply to virtual worlds (see Lastowska & Hunter 2004; Kerr 2008; Viersma and Keupink 2006), the state (public prosecutor) can under circumstances intervene with virtual world actions. This brings us to the Dutch court cases in which was decided that theft of virtual property is possible.

3 Virtual Theft Case Law

In November 2007, I delivered an in-company tutorial on law and virtual worlds for the Information Technology and Intellectual Property section of an Amsterdam law firm. We had quite some discussion on unfair terms of services by virtual

---

[9]For instance, Kevin Alderman needed two sub poenas and used a private investigator to finally find out who was behind the avatar Catteneo, who was infringing on his virtual beds (see Reuters 2008).

world producers,[10] the far stretching intellectual property claims of these same producers,[11] and the issue of virtual property as well as theft of virtual objects. As a nice co-incidence, on that same day a TV news program broadcasted an item on the arrest of a youngster being accused of stealing virtual items out of the Habbo Hotel. This case got quite some coverage, also outside the Netherlands,[12] for there was no precedent yet of someone being accused of virtual theft.

Illustrative in this respect is one of the most famous virtual law cases on the Chinese gamer Qui Chengwei killing his friend Zhu Caoyuan. In that case, a virtual Sabre sword was sold and the Chinese police was not willing to handle the case because according to Chinese Penal law virtual objects could not be stolen.[13]

Interestingly enough, when discussing the Dutch cases on virtual theft during the Heidelberg meeting *Virtual worlds and Criminality* in January 2009 that led to this book, the German scholars were quite firm about penalizing stealing virtual objects under German law: impossible. Their argument was straightforward. ′Sache′ is tangible, only tangible objects can be stolen. Virtual objects do not fall under that category, for they are intangible. Therefore, in German law, you cannot qualify the taking away of virtual objects as theft. In addition, Peter S. Jenkins (in reply to Lodder 2008b, TerraNova blog) states:

> Property rights only exist due to the coercive powers of the state, which must be convinced that there are valid socioeconomic and public policy reasons for it to expend its resources on upholding/enforcing such rights. In a virtual world where the taken object can be instantly replaced (as well as deleted from the taker's account) due to a code entry, it may be difficult to convince a court that such reasons exist.

Greg Lastowka does not agree, but regarding prosecution he is also somewhat sceptical (in reply to Lodder 2008b, TerraNova blog):

> I don't think I would disagree if you were just arguing that prosecutors would not put policing virtual theft high on their to do list.

The Dutch prosecutors did prosecute in two virtual theft cases. I will discuss the arguments used in the Dutch course cases on virtual theft. In the Habbo hotel case several suspects were prosecuted, and eventual three largely similar cases were

---

[10]The most famous one in this respect probably is that your account can be terminated at any time, for any reason or *no reason at all* (for example Article 11.6 of Linden Lab's TOS).

[11]The producers claim e.g. to have intellectual property rights even on in game moral rights and conversations between participants (for example Article XV TOS of World of Warcraft).

[12]For instance, the BBC reported: 'A Dutch teenager has been arrested for allegedly stealing virtual furniture from "rooms" in Habbo Hotel, a 3D social networking website'. (http://news.bbc.co.uk/2/hi/technology/7094764.stm. Same problem, the link to the website does not work. See also Thomasson 2007, Duranske 2007b and Christensen 2007).

[13]It was in fact this case that raise my interest in Law and Virtual worlds. One of my students during that time, Menno Briet, pointed me at this case and suggested that virtual worlds could be an interesting area for applying online dispute resolution (ODR).

ruled.[14] This was on 2 April 2009. Although the Habbo Hotel case was the first one in which virtual theft was prosecuted, the Amsterdam court was not the first to rule on theft on virtual items. A later case was ruled earlier, namely on 21 October 2008. I will start the discussion with the latter case.

3.1 Virtual Theft in Runescape

The case on Runescape[15] is one that 'broke' the magic circle at the outset, since *real*, physical violence was used. This is a clear example where conflicts about virtual items cannot be resolved in-game. Not only because the crucial acts took place offline, but in particular because of the nature of those acts.

On 5 September 2007, the 15-year-old main suspect and his 14-year-old companion planned to rob the Runescape account of a 13-year-old boy who was quite good in this online game. They decided[16] to take him to their apartment the next day, and even discussed that if this 13-year-old boy would not be willing to co-operate they would use violence.

One of the suspects (further: offenders) indicated during hearings that he was jealous because he used to be virtually richer than the victim but no longer was. A couple of days before the incident the victim had found a dead man (virtual!) who was very rich. He could take the items of the dead man and became wealthy: richer than the suspect. The suspect asked the victim several times whether he could get some items or money, but the victim did not want to share his virtual items with the eventual offender.

On 6 September 2007, the two offenders arrived in the apartment with the 13-year-old victim. He was not prepared to log into Runescape and hand over virtual money and items to the offenders, so they started to beat and kick him, and also tried to strangle him. When all this violence did not have the desired effect, both went to the kitchen and grabbed some knives, and made threatening gestures. One of the offenders had a big butcher's knife and started to scream "I kill you". Afterwards they put back the knives, and asked the victim to log in. By that time the victim was so scared that he did log in. He logged into the computer of the living room. In the meantime, one of the offenders logged into another computer and fought with his avatar against the avatar of the victim. In the end the offenders got a very valuable amulet as well as a mask, and the coins of the victim's account.

[14]The online database http://rechtspraak.nl/default.htm (which includes Dutch case law) contains only a selection of cases, so there might have been one or two more cases on the Habbo Hotel theft, but this is not relevant for the discussion of the arguments used in this case.

[15]RuneScape is a massive 3d multiplayer adventure, with monsters to kill, quests to complete, and treasure to win (http://www.Runescape.com).

[16]Contrary to how physical it would get, they made their plans for virtual theft using MSN.

3.2 Court of Leeuwarden October 21, 2008[17]

The main charge was not ordinary theft (Article 310 Dutch Penal Code – maximum penalty 4 years), but theft in combination with violence and conducted by more than one person (Article 312, subsection 2 under 2 Dutch Penal Code – maximum penalty 12 years).[18] The acts also qualify as black-mail or extortion (Article 317 Dutch Penal Code – maximum penalty in combination with the same subsection of Article 312 also 12 years). Kaspersen has a point when he argues that this criminal act is more on point in the current situation.[19] Luckily, the Court of Leeuwarden convicted on the basis of theft, because, to my knowledge, this is the first case law on an issue discussed for long: whether the taking away of virtual item qualifies as theft.

In the judgement the Court decided that the offenders were guilty of theft based on the following arguments[20]:

- The purpose of the Article on theft is to protect capital (assets, resources, money).
- The question should be answered whether virtual items are goods in terms of the theft article. The following issues should be considered:
  - *Does the item has value?* Virtual goods of online games like Runescape have become important to large group of people, and have value for many online gamers. The more goods a player possesses, the stronger a player is. Moreover, virtual goods are bought and sold, e.g. via internet or on the schoolyard. In the present case it is clear that the mask and amulet had value for the victim as well as the suspects.
  - *Tangible?* It follows from previous case law that a stolen good not necessarily has to be tangible, also non-tangible items can be considered goods in the meaning of the Theft Article. On 23 May 1921, the Dutch Supreme Court ruled that electricity can be stolen, and in the 1980s/1990s several cases were on stealing of money on account (transferable money).
  - *Taking away?* An important characteristic in case of stealing is that the one who takes away gets the power over the object, and the one from who the objects is stolen loses this power. The possession should be transferred from one to the other. Possession in penal law means actual power. In case law, it has been decided that you do not lose actual power in case of a pin code, computer data, and (this last one is arguably, ARL) minute account on a

[17]http://www.rechtspraak.nl/ljn.asp?ljn=BG0939.

[18]Note that convictions never reach the maximum in cases such as theft, and the penalties for minors are less severe anyway.

[19]Kaspersen argued in his farewell address 'Kalme chaos van het internet' (March 13, 2009) that the Leeuwarden Court made a mistake by qualifying those acts as theft in combination with violence, and indicated that this should have been qualified as extortion.

[20]What follows below follows the main arguments used by the Court, to which I added additional explanatory remarks where necessary.

phone subscription. In the current case, the victim had actual power over the amulet and the mask. Possession of virtual goods can be transferred, from one account to another account. In this case the possession was transferred from the victim to the offender(s). The victim lost actual power, and the offenders obtained actual power over the amulet and the mask.

The Court decided that the amulet and mask met the above criteria, and therefore qualified as good in the sense of the Theft Article. The most controversial element has actually not been addressed explicitly, namely the tangible nature of goods. Reference to prior case law sufficed here. On the following grounds the Supreme Court decided in the electricity case (1921) that electricity can be stolen.

1. Electricity can only be observed in connection with a physical object, but through human intervention electricity can be transported and accumulated.
2. Electricity is generated by human.
3. Electricity has economic value.

Since the aim of the theft Article is to protect property and the taking away of goods is penalized without making explicitly clear what falls under the scope of goods, because of the above observations (1–3) electricity should also fall under the scope of this Theft article.

One of the lines of defence was that what happened in Runescape was according to the rules of the game. So, the attorney used the Magic Circle to support his claim: if the game allows it, you should not apply legal rules. He is right in the sense that what actually happened in-game did not violate the rules. However, the Court rightly observed that the criminal acts of the suspects did not take place in the context of the game, and therefore the rules of the game do not apply to those acts.

Finally, the court ruled that the suspects were guilty of theft. The 15-year-old was sentenced to 200 h service, and the 14-year-old to 160 h.

3.3 Court of Appeal Leeuwarden November 10, 2009[21]

From a virtual law perspective, this is not relevant, but nonetheless interesting is the argument in appeal that the suspects were not informed that they had a right to an attorney during hearings (based on European Court of Human Rights November 27, 2008 ruling in the Salduz case, and the similar Dutch Supreme Court decision of June 30, 2009[22]). The Court of Appeal accepted the argument and decided that as a consequence the statements of the suspects could not be used to proof their guilt. However, what the suspects stated about the other suspect could be used, so in the

[21]http://www.rechtspraak.nl/ljn.asp?ljn=BK2773.

[22]http://www.rechtspraak.nl/ljn.asp?ljn=BH3079.

end this successful argument had no consequence regarding their conviction: they were found guilty based on the testimony of the other.

The other appeal argument was that the mask and amulet are neither tangible nor have any economic value, and therefore are no goods. The court states that the criterion of tangibility has been left since the – above mentioned – Electricity case in 1921, and that over the years the concept of economic value has been changed to value for the possessor of the item. In the current case, it is very clear that the item was of value for the victim, and both suspects. The victim had indicated that he was very rich in Runescape and almost unbeatable. Because of his power, he was afraid of being hacked and changed his password every 3 days. The Court also states that the value originates during play, after spending both time and effort.

Based on the above observation, the Court also comes to the conclusion that virtual items are goods in the sense of Article 310 on theft. Again the Court stresses that what happened in real life is not foreseen in the rules of the game. This case is not about virtual acts in a virtual world per se, but about factual acts that influence a virtual world.

Another argument by the defence is that the items are not in possession of the players, but that they only have a right to use the items. They state that the online game and everything that happens within the virtual worlds remains in the possession of the producer of the game (Jagex Ltd., UK). See also Greg Lastowka (in reply to Lodder 2008b, TerraNova blog):

> Second, it is premised on a private software structure that is malleable and could, potentially, be used to restore the virtual property at issue to the true owner.

John (in reply to Lodder 2008b, TerraNova blog):

> The company, after all, is effectively god in their little virtual world. If they recognize it as hacking they just need to transfer the item back and place some sort of punishment on the hacker. (. . .) The only way something can be lost in a virtual world is if the god allows it to be lost.

Backrazor (in reply to Lodder 2008b, TerraNova blog):

> . . .) Most devs / managers do indeed claim ownership of all the objects in their game, at the point of Eula or ToS. So in theory, this impedes concepts of virtual theft, since the objects don't belong to the victim in the first place

The Court states that this interpretation of the term "belongs to" is too restricted.[23] A player has the factual and exclusive power over the items in his possession. Only the victim could, after logging into Runescape, use the amulet and mask. Because of the theft, he no longer has exclusive actual power. The fact that the game Runescape has an owner and/or producer is not relevant. For instance, the owner of a passport is the state, but this passport can be stolen *from* the citizen to which this passport belongs. Although the Court is right, the difference of course is that the State cannot give back the original passport, but only give a new one.

[23] ". . . taking away a good that belongs to. . .".

The Court of Appeal repeats that the criterion used in case law that the good should leave the actual power of the one from whom it is stolen is met in this case. This is different in case of taking away of software, computer data, and pin code. (Note that different from the first instance court the minute account on a phone subscription is not mentioned.)

Based on all this, the court decides that the taking away of the amulet and mask can be qualified as theft. The court also indicates that as a consequence of the digitalisation of our society a virtual reality cannot in all respects be considered as pure illusion, which would exclude committing of criminal acts.

In addition to 160 h service, the Court of Appeal also – because of the severity of the act – condemns the offenders to 1 month of youth detention.

3.4 *Virtual Theft in Habbo Hotel: Court of Amsterdam 2009*[24]

The Habbo Hotel was quite different from the Runescape case for various reasons. It concerned a group of youngsters that in between December 3, 2006 and February 18, 2007 took away several items from the Habbo accounts of other players. They operated by so-called phishing using a fake site of Hotmail. They sent e-mail messages to Habbo Hotel users with a link to the fake Hotmail site. After retrieving the password of Hotmail, they logged in and sent an e-mail to Sulake (the producer of Habbo Hotel) to ask for a new password for their Habbo account. After receiving this, they logged into Habbo hotel and transferred items, basically virtual furniture, to their own accounts.

Before going to the police, the producer of the game asked the 'phishers' to stop. Only after several warnings Sulake decided to go to the police, and reported hacking of accounts. The actual victims also went to the police and they reported theft of virtual items.

The – at least three – suspects were all convicted. Interestingly enough, the judge did not pay any attention to the question whether the taking away of virtual furniture qualifies as theft. He simply indicated that those items were taken from the accounts of others, and concludes that the suspects are guilty of theft.

More consideration is put into the hacking. The attorney argued that hacking is a lex specialis of theft and as a consequence being guilty of hacking excludes being guilty of theft. See also Vili Lehdonvirta (in reply to Lodder 2008b, TerraNova blog):

> One could argue that the article on theft in the Criminal Code is not necessary, for a possible case of theft is always preceded by unlawful hacking. The problem with this approach is that only the operator will then have standing to sue

---

[24]http://www.rechtspraak.nl/ljn.asp?ljn=BH9789; http://www.rechtspraak.nl/ljn.asp?ljn=BH9790; http://www.rechtspraak.nl/ljn.asp?ljn=BH9791.

In case of hacking, however, the central concept is not "take away" but "taking over, tap and record". All those acts refer to copying. If data are taken over, they remain in the possession of the one from whom they were taken. This is essentially different from "taking away" in which case the actual power is lost.

The defence that the goal of the game is to acquire as many furniture as possible was easily put aside. What the offenders did is disproportionate, and completely out of the context of the game. It has simply nothing to do with the rules of the Habbo Hotel.

4 Conclusion

It is common knowledge that where people meet conflicts can occur. This is not different for virtual worlds. What makes virtual worlds special is that they resemble in many ways the real world. Not surprisingly, also state norms can be used to resolve virtual world conflicts.

In this paper, it has been argued that irrespective of the nature of the norm, be it the rules of the game, the social norms or the legal norms, the first step should be to try to resolve the conflict amicably through direct negotiation, preferably in-world. This is in line with what the Magic Circle metaphor aims to express, viz. that the outside world should not intervene with virtual worlds. However, sometimes it is necessary to apply legal norms, and/or use state organized legal procedures. In private law, there have been several law suits, in particular in the United States, but almost all of them were settled. So there are not so many precedents yet. Another example of norms which violation should be approached from outside the virtual world is penal norms. We should consider for each case whether violation of criminal norms take place, and if so, whether it is sensible to prosecute.

The Dutch prosecutors considered the behaviour surrounding the taking away of virtual objects serious enough to start a case. This case law on virtual theft is interesting, for it demonstrates that penal norms can be violated in virtual worlds. The Runescape case is somewhat a-typical, for it involved serious physical violence, but the Habbo theft was truly taking place online only. Future will tell if more criminal oriented cases follow. Because of the volume of the virtual world activities, I expect this will be the case.

References

Castronova E (2005) The Horde is evil. TerraNova blog. http://terranova.blogs.com/terra_nova/2005/12/the_horde_is_ev.html, accessed on 15 January 2010

Christensen B (2007) Virtual theft from Habbo Hotel. http://www.technovelgy.com/ct/Science-Fiction-News.asp?NewsNum=1310, accessed on 15 January 2010

Duranske B (2007a) Weblog: virtually blind. http://virtuallyblind.com/2007/04/26/quicklinks-the-magic-circle, accessed on 15 January 2010

Duranske B (2007b) Dutch police arrest seventeen-year-old for $5800 virtual furniture theft at Habbo Hotel. http://virtuallyblind.com/2007/11/14/habbo-theft/, accessed on 15 January 2010

Fairfield J (2009) The magic circle. Vanderbilt J Entertain Technol Law. http://ssrn.com/abstract=1304234, accessed on 15 January 2010

Katsh E, Rifkin J (2001) Online dispute resolution: resolving conflicts in cyberspace. Wiley, New York

Kerr, Orin S. (2008), Criminal Law in Virtual Worlds. University of Chicago Legal Forum, Forthcoming; GWU Law School Public Law Research Paper No. 391. Available at SSRN: http://ssrn.com/abstract=1097392, accessed on 15 January 2010

Kirby C (2009) Avatars, attorneys in new world of virtual law. San Francisco Chronicle. http://articles.sfgate.com/2009-04-27/business/17194388_1_second-life-virtual-worlds-san-francisco-s-linden-lab, accessed on 15 January 2010

Kuznicki J (2007) Virtual fascists and the value of private property. http://www.positiveliberty.com/2007/01/virtual-fascists-and-the-value-of-private-property.html, accessed on 15 January 2010

Lastowska, F. Gregory & Hunter, Dan (2004) Virtual Crimes, 49 New York Law School Law Review 293 (Institute for Information Law and Policy Symposium) 2004 http://www.nyls.edu/pdfs/v49n1p293-316.pdf, accessed on 15 January 2010

Linden Lab´s (2010) Terms of Service. http://secondlife.com/corporate/tos.php#tos10, accessed on 15 January 2010

Lodder AR (2007) Short note on virtual law classes: second life and other three dimensional visual worlds next phase for online dispute resolution? In: Lodder AR, Rule C, Zeleznikow J (eds) Proceedings 4th International Workshop on ODR. San Jose, pp 59–62. http://ssrn.com/abstract=1014845, accessed on 15 January 2010

Lodder AR (2008a) Why not qualify the taking away of virtual objects as theft? 08.02.2008. TerraNova blog. http://terranova.blogs.com/terra_nova/2008/02/why-not-qualify.html#more, accessed on 15 January 2010

Lodder AR (2008b) Why not qualify the taking away of virtual objects as theft? 22.02.2008. TerraNova blog. http://terranova.blogs.com/terra_nova/2008/02/why-not-qualify.html#more, accessed on 15 January 2010

Lodder AR, van Kokswijk J (2008) Recht in online reality: de juridische werkelijkheid in fantasie werelden [Law in online reality: legal reality in fantasy worlds]. Paris uitgevers, Deventer

Lodder AR, Zeleznikow J (2010) Technology enhanced dispute resolution through the use of information technology. Cambridge University Press, Cambridge

Reuters E (2007a) SL business sues for copyright infringement. http://secondlife.reuters.com/stories/2007/07/03/sl-business-sues-for-copyright-infringement/, accessed on 15 January 2010

Reuters E (2007b) Judge rules against 'one-sided' TOS in Bragg lawsuit. http://secondlife.reuters.com/stories/2007/05/31/judge-rules-against-one-sided-tos-in-bragg-lawsuit/, accessed on 15 January 2010

Reuters E (2008) Volkov catteneo: Yes, I am Robert Leatherwood. http://secondlife.reuters.com/stories/2008/03/06/volkov-catteneo-yes-i-am-robert-leatherwood/, accessed on 15 January 2010

Thomasson E (2007) Dutch police arrest teenage online furniture thief. http://uk.reuters.com/article/idUKL1453844620071114, accessed on 15 January 2010

Viersma M, Keupink B (2006) 'Virtuele criminaliteit: all in the game', in: A.R. Lodder (red.), *Recht in een virtuele wereld: juridische aspecten van massive multiplayer online role playing games*, NVvIR, Elsevier, p. 41–59

World of Warcraft® (2009) Terms of use agreement. http://www.wow-europe.com/en/legal/termsofuse.html, accessed on 15 January 2010

Responsibility under Criminal Law in Virtual Worlds

Kai Cornelius

Abstract Criminal acts can pay off in the virtual world just as in the real world. Virtual values created or traded in the virtual world, which can be changed into real money, provide incentives for committing all kinds of offences. Business transactions conducted in the virtual world by delivering mere virtual goods or services create new possibilities of money laundering. These possibilities are magnified by the worldwide accessibility of the virtual currency.

Virtual criminality whose effects remain in the virtual world, in the classification used here (In-World ←→ In-World), should not trigger remedies under the criminal law. The action of a User must be considered from a Real-World perspective and the extent to which this action might constitute an offence must be ascertained. On the User-to-User level, the classic computer offences such as data espionage (unauthorized access to a computer) and data tampering, as well as intellectually communicated offences such as duress and insult have to be considered. The application of fraud and extortion laws to virtual-world crime is less clear-cut, as it is doubtful whether the virtual objects involved in the alleged "fraud" or "extortion" really can be understood as assigned to the assets of any user. An argument in favor of considering virtual objects as assigned to a user's assets is that the user has a right to use and possibly even sell the virtual object. An argument against is that the Terms of Service regularly provide that the operator reserves the right to cancel the user's account (and any assets within it) without granting a material compensation for any losses.

Those engaged in making or distributing child pornography have found a new way to commit crimes through 3D-Worlds: the presentation of sexual acts using avatars with childlike appearances. Different legal systems provide vastly different regulations to address such practices. The divergent value standards of the different

K. Cornelius (✉)
Institute for German, European and International Criminal Law, University of Heidelberg, Heidelberg, Germany
e-mail: Cornelius@jurs.uni-heidelberg.de

K. Cornelius and D. Hermann (eds.), *Virtual Worlds and Criminality*,
DOI 10.1007/978-3-642-20823-2_7,

legal systems become obvious with regard to not only pornography but also such crimes as incitement to hatred and raise the question of which standards should apply in a global setting. In addition, there is a new phenomenon of "cyber mobbing" which merits analysis as to what its effects are and whether any legal action is needed. As long as cyber mobbing is not regarded as duress or persecution, which is a precondition for stalking, it cannot be punished according to German criminal law. Any duties (to take or refrain from specified acts) arising from the Provider–User relationship also requires discussion, especially with regard to whether a stronger legal involvement is needed to prevent specified offences.

The establishment of virtual worlds increases the pressure to coordinate the fight against cyber criminality, which is already necessary because of the internet without borders. This coordination must be followed by further efforts of the international community of states on different (national, supranational, and international) levels in order to develop generally acknowledged "cores of injustice" (Unrechtskerne).

1 Introduction

Crime has arrived in virtual worlds. And it is no wonder, since Criminals always follow the money! It is now possible to create virtual values that can be exchanged for real money[1] and that possibility is a strong incentive for committing a diverse range of crimes. With nearly half a billion registered users in virtual worlds[2] and a turnover of real money for virtual goods ("Real Money Trade" or "RMT")[3] rising from nearly 2 billion dollars in the end of 2007 (cf. ENISA 2008, p. 3) to 3 billion dollars in 2009 (source KZero 2010), this is a serious subject (cf. Koch 2006; Trump and Wedemeyer 2006, p. 397; Habel 2008, p. 71; Klickermann 2007, p. 766 and Psczolla 2008, p. 5f).

One example of the explosiveness of the RMT issue is China's prohibition against the exchange of virtual currencies for real money in order to guard against the danger of creating a secondary currency in the country (although the exchange of virtual *objects* for real money is explicitly excluded from this prohibition). Regardless of whether the prohibition is sound policy, this much is true: the Chinese

[1]This explains the existence of such companies as *Internet Gaming to entertainment* (www.ige.com/about.html) as *Gameeconomy* (www.gameeconomy.de), which make available a platform on which users can maximize trade and exchange articles from the largest number of different virtual worlds.

[2]According to the consulting firm *KZero kursiv*, number of registered users of virtual worlds has grown from 417 million in the first quarter of 2009 to 579 million in the second quarter (see Virtual World News 2009).

[3]To the various manifestations of the RMT see Lehdonvirta (2008); cf. also Nänni (2008) who makes a distinction between a primary market (sales of virtual objects by the operating authority) and a secondary market (sales of virtual objects by the users).

government has good reason to take serious notice. China has the world's largest population of Internet users, with 384 million people online by the end of 2009.[4] The virtual money trade in China topped several billion yuan in 2008 after rising around 20% annually (see Xinhua 2009).

For the purposes of this paper, a virtual world is a persistent, computer-generated environment through which a user can interact with a huge number of other users (see Nänni 2008, p. 3; for other approaches to definitions cf. Bell 2008). The key distinction of a virtual world from traditional computer games lies in this persistency. While a computer game may be switched on or off by its user at will, the virtual world is preserved and is able to change according to its underlying rules. Although a single user is able to log on or off at any time, he[5] has no control over the progress of the virtual world and the way it evolves as a result of the actions of other users while he or she is logged off (see Nänni 2008, p. 3; confer for the functionality of virtual worlds also Habel 2008, pp. 71/72; Psczolla 2008, p. 5). When a user is logged on, he or she moves with his or her avatar through the artificially generated environment in search of various acquisitions and experiences. The aim is to improve the avatar's status and capabilities and acquire things such as new clothes, pieces of equipment, or weapons. The level of development the avatar achieves determines what assignments the user can solve or what "social" status he or she enjoys in the virtual world via his or her avatar (cf. Psczolla 2008, p. 5).

But what happens technically, if a user decides to arm his or her avatar with a virtual sword and to spend money to buy it? What does it mean to "buy" a "sword" in the virtual world? What does the user really acquire? The users of virtual worlds perceive objects (such as swords) as images on their monitors which are formations of pixel generated by data. The appearance and the qualities of the virtual object are defined by an entry in one database (an item-database), while an entry in another database (a character-database) establishes which virtual objects are assigned to a particular user (cf. Nänni 2009, p.4). These data are stored by the service provider on central servers (see Psczolla 2008, p. 5).

Against this background, legally important questions arise. Which criminal offences come into consideration? Fraud can be as lucrative in virtual worlds such as *World of Warcraft, Entropia Universe,* or *Second Life* as it is in the real world. The settlement of a business transaction in the virtual world with the delivery of purely virtual goods or services presents new possibilities for money laundering in the real world. Other crimes common to virtual worlds include content offences such as glorification of violence, insult, defamation, incitement to hatred, or virtual child pornography.

Other criminal law provisions, like those covering data espionage, alteration of data and computer sabotage, also exist that prohibit the stealing of virtual objects,

---

[4]Data available at http://www.internetworldstats.com/asia.htm

[5]The masculine form is used hereinafter solely in the interest of readability

but they do not protect against the very real financial loss that can result from the loss of the virtual object itself. Rather, these provisions are aimed at protecting the individuals' privacy interests or their interest in the proper functioning by their data systems.

This paper will be focused on the very new problems arising in the context of virtual worlds in contrast to "normal" Internet use. Therefore, cybercrime law provisions covering data espionage, alteration of data, and computer sabotage, and content offences such as the glorification of violence, insult, defamation, and incitement to hatred will not be analyzed at length.

The first part of the paper will discuss violations of the legally protected rights of outsiders to the online world, in particular copyright infringements, trademark violations, money laundering, and terrorism financing.

The second part analyzes offences within the user-to-user relationship. The discussion will examine offences involving virtual assets, such as fraud and blackmail, with a special focus on the limits of legal protection accorded to "unstable" virtual assets (as defined hereafter), as well as virtual child pornography. As a starting point, this discussion considers whether virtual world actions should be judged entirely from the perspective of the virtual world or from the perspective of the real world. This paper proposes the term "virtureal" rather than "virtual" for describing crimes arising from virtual world use and their injurious effects in the real world. Additionally, the legal meaning of the virtual world's internal rules is considered.

The article concentrates on the German Criminal Law, but – to highlight the differences in various legal systems, especially in the field of content offences – also pays attention to issues of criminal liability for virtual child pornography under US law.

2 Violations of the Legally Protected Rights of Outsiders

The first category of potential criminal violations examined in this article involves the users of online worlds and the effects of their online activities on external third parties (i.e., outsiders to the online world). Four types of criminal conduct are particularly significant in this context and are therefore being examined below: copyright infringements, trademark violations, money laundering, and terrorism financing.

2.1 Copyright Infringements

The extent to which the private law of copyrights applies to virtual worlds has not yet been established. Even the preliminary question of whether copyrights can be infringed by representing images of real-world objects in a virtual world setting

("In-World") is very much open. In the virtual world, illustrations that evoke the exact textures of real objects or of real structures (such as the Cologne Cathedral) can be considered as works protected by copyright law (see Hoeren 2010, Sect. 9 marginal number 261f; Wandtke et al. 2009, Sect. 2 marginal number 152f; Psczolla 2008, pp. 23f; Geis and Geis 2007, pp. 721, 723, decision from the LG Köln *(District Court)* 2008, p. 556). However, to date, there are no internationally defined standards for determining the threshold level of originality (in German: Schöpfungshöhe) that is required for copyright protection. Thus, the legal status of illustrations in virtual worlds is unclear.[6]

In Germany, the copyright law as applied to virtual worlds has developed somewhat. It has been established that the creation – with graphics tools – of illustrations in virtual worlds (as is the case with *Second Life*) is eligible for protection by copyright law under certain circumstances (cf. Rippert and Weimer 2007, p. 272, 277; Psczolla 2008, pp. 558, 559). There are two classes of copyrightable works: (1) "design" or "applied art" (angewandte Kunst), and (2) "fine art" (bildende Kunst) (cf. BGH *(Federal High Court of Justice)* 1972, pp. 38, 39). "Applied art" is a design that serves a practical purpose, whereas "fine art" comprises everything else, including literary works. The threshold of originality required to trigger copyright protection for fine art is low; even very simple creations, known in German as "Kleine Münze", ("Small Coin"), can meet the requirements (see Schulze 2004, Sect. 2 marginal number 153; Dreyer et al. 2004, Sect. 2 marginal number 221). The requirements for design are set much higher (cf. BGH 1995, pp. 581, 582). Only design creations that are very high above average in quality and uniqueness are considered to meet the standards for copyright protection. It is the *purpose* served by a work of applied art that is the primary factor separating it from a work of fine art (OLG (*Higher Regional Court*) 2008, pp. 140, 142).

As an example in case law, an illustration of the *Cologne Cathedral* in a virtual world was not considered protectable under German copyright law. The District Court reviewing the *Cologne* case has classified the "replica" of the Cologne Cathedral in Second Life as a work of applied art, because it serves the purpose "to exhaust . . . the full potential of virtual worlds and to be of social and economic use to all participants of the project." (Köln 2008, pp. 556, 558)[7].

This characterization might also apply to a majority of virtual creations. Virtual objects mostly have a "purpose" in the virtual world. The purpose of the avatar is to navigate through the virtual space. The representation of a real-world company in a virtual world serves as a marketing instrument. Therefore, such virtual objects should be categorized as a work of applied art, under the *Cologne* standard. Only very special individual and artistic creations will reach the high requirements for

---

[6]This concept in copyright law is used in important legislations, see since 1991 for the United States *Feist* v. *Rural*, 499 U.S. 340 (1991). Another concept is the so-called sweat of the brow doctrine, which grants copyright protection based on how much labor and diligence it took to create a work, rather than or in addition to how original a work is.

[7]Different opinion Büchner (2008, pp. 425, 426).

copyright protection for this class of works. If, however, a virtual object reaches the threshold of originality, it would enjoy copyright protection, so that the application of copy programs such as "Copybot" to duplicate that virtual object would be a copyright infringement (cf. Geis and Geis 2007, pp. 721, 723f).

Some criminal liabilities for copyright violations are provided for in the accessory criminal provisions of the German Copyright Act (Sects. 106ff. UrhG). However, liability under these provisions is triggered only after the preliminary question is answered as to whether the civil law copyright protections apply to an illustration in a virtual world. If they do, then criminal law protections will also apply and punishments can be imposed for the duplication, distribution, or public reproduction of a virtual creation without the approval of its creator or other properly designated the beneficiary of its copyright (except in certain legally admitted cases) (cf. for the use of Cheatbots Wieduwilt 2008, p. 715). For this reason, whether unauthorized duplications of virtual-world creations are punishable as copyright violations is a question that cannot be answered in general terms, but only on an individual basis, taking into account such standards as the threshold of originality, when appropriate, to determine whether a civil-law copyright exists. As such, virtual objects that have a use purpose (such as avatars or buildings) will enjoy civil-law copyright protection – and, consequently, criminal law protection against the intentional violation of such copyrights – only when their purpose or design is sufficiently specialized or unique. In the case of generic, simply designed avatars and buildings, wherein even unauthorized duplication is not punishable, the derivative crimes of spreading or public reproduction will not be punishable either.

2.2 *Trademark Violations*

In virtual worlds, unauthorized use of real-world trademarks – for example, by using digital pictures or imitations of real and virtual works without suitable authorization from the owner of the trademark – is fairly common (see Klickermann 2007, pp. 766, 767; Duranske 2008, pp. 149f.; cf. also Hartmann 2007). The protection of the German trademark law that applies in the real world is also valid in virtual worlds. However, it is still unclear whether the protections apply across the real-virtual divide. For instance, the question of whether a virtual-world simulation of a real-world object or image (such as a visually accurate virtual replica of a real car model including the right brand symbols) is a trademark infringement, has not yet been finally established. In case of a trademark infringement, the violator must count on facing considerable actions for injunctive relief and claims for tort damages. If a virtual simulation of a real-world object is found to have a use in commercial dealings, the application of the criminal provisions of the German Trademark Act (Sect. 143ff. MarkenG) is possible.

2.3 Money Laundering

Money laundering is a supranational crime (cf. Chaikin 1991, pp. 415f). Many descriptions of money laundering draw on the definition by the American *President's Commission on Organized Crime* in its interim report: *The Cash Connection: Organized Crime, Financial Institutions, and Money Laundering*: "Money Laundering is the process by which one conceals the existence, illegal source, or illegal application of income, and then disguises that income to make it appear legitimate" (cf. US Presidents Commission on Organized Crime/United States 1984, p. 7; Kern 1993, p. 17; Stessens 2000, p. 83).

Virtual worlds offer the money launderer an easy way to exchange or transfer virtual values for real currency.[8] This is possible largely for two reasons. First, In-World transactions are subject to very minimal legal or governmental controls. Second, it is possible that the percentage paid to move currency into and out of virtual worlds is so low that the efficiencies rate can be from 90 to 98% (see Boyd and Moersfelder 2007, pp. 4, 5). However, the volume of worldwide transactions in virtual currencies (2 billion US-dollars of RMT in 2007 and 3 billion US-dollars of RMT in 2009) (see ENISA 2008, p. 3) is still marginal, considering that the 2008 gross domestic product (GDP) was 14,441 trillion US-dollars for the United States and 3,673 trillion US-dollars for Germany (according to the International Monetary Fund 2010). However, as the economic importance of virtual worlds grows, so will the amount of dirty money that gets laundered through them and the diversity of possible ways to keep the money-laundering processes undetectable.

The usual procedure of money laundering can be divided into three phases, *Placement Stage, Layering,* and *Integration*, which often overlap and are not readily separated from each other (cf. Buchanan 2004, pp. 115, 117; Hoyer and Klos 2001, p. 9; Jason-Lloyd 1997, pp. 1f). Nevertheless, each phase gives rise to sufficiently discrete issues to warrant a separate discussion, as provided in the following three Sects. 2.3.1–2.3.3. Each of these subsections is intended as a simplified overview of what in reality is a highly complex process, to develop a feeling for the possibilities available to money-launderers in virtual worlds.

---

[8] See United States Department of State: Bureau for International Narcotics and Law Enforcement Affairs (2009, p. 6). "Such capabilities in virtual world games have potential implications for money laundering and other financial crimes. It is now possible to set up an account by furnishing false identification, fund the account with illicit proceeds, and have a co-conspirator in a criminal enterprise on the other side of the world withdraw funds. For example, in 2008 South Korean authorities arrested a group involved with the laundering of $38 million in virtual currencies." Equally Choo and Smith (2007, pp. 37, 49): "Risks of money laundering will increase as MMOG and MMORPG sites emerge as a vehicle for money laundering online." Cf. also von Heintschel-Heinegg (2010, § 261 marginal number 4.2).

2.3.1 Placement Stage

The first step in money laundering entails placing the illegal money somewhere. This phase is alternatively called "placement stage" (Jason-Lloyd 1997, pp. 1f) or "prewash cycle" (Bülte 2006, p. 166). It is the intersection between the illegal and legal financial markets and is marked by changing bulk cash amounts derived from criminal activities into more portable and less suspicious forms. The cash is then either converted to "book money" (e.g., payment on a bank account) or is declared as legal income from a regular source such as a shop.[9] In this way, the illicit money succeeds in infiltrating the mainstream financial system (cf. Hoyer and Klos 2001, p. 12). This process requires financial institutions or trustees with a willingness to cooperate in the process. Consequently, capital exports for the placement stage take place mainly to countries with lax regulations of the banking and finance sectors. This phase involves the greatest risks for money launderers. It is during this phase that the money-laundering activity has the highest chance of being discovered by law enforcement authorities (see Buchanan 2004, pp. 115, 117; Bülte 2006, p. 166).

There are a number of ways to involve the virtual world in the placement phase. One is direct participation in the virtual economy by running a company In-World. But also a no controllable transfer of assets is conceivable: An account with virtual values (money or objects) is charged and then the account dates are sent to another person. The consignee of these account dates can sit at the other end of the world. He or she has full control over the account and can even change virtual values in real money. For a surveillant in the virtual world, it looks as if there is every time the same person (the accountholder) to act.

2.3.2 Layering

In the next step, the money launderer tries to blur the tracks of the money in such a way that the so-called paper trail[10] between the various steps in the process is interrupted (see Hoyer and Klos 2001, pp. 12f). In this, the "Layering" phase – sometimes called the "main washing cycle" – a variety of transactions are carried out on an international level and/or in offshore centers, so that the movement of the illicit money becomes too complicated to track. Such transactions have taken many forms. One widely used transaction is the over-invoicing of the value of imported goods. Another method is the use of gold (as an ingot, ring, bracelet, pendant, or ornament), simply because a single piece of gold can be changed many times in order to disguise its original form without any significant change in its worth (cf. Jason-Lloyd 1997, pp. 1f).

---

[9]Detailed description about the methods (e.g., also fraud, structuring/smurfing, gambling and the buying of life insurances) in Schneider et al. (2006, pp. 49f).

[10]Paper trail stands for records about business processes, which allow the tracking of financial transactions (see Bülte 2006, p. 165).

Virtual worlds are perfectly suited to be used in this main washing cycle. Transactions between avatars are practically never watched by third parties in the real world. A legitimization of the capital transfer can happen, for example, by the purchase of a virtual object or property. For example, organized crime groups can purchase virtual properties in the virtual worlds worth 1,000 Linden dollars (the currency of the virtual world *Second Life*), but actually pay 2 million dollars in cash. Colluding avatars (controlled by criminals) can also launder proceeds of illicit activities in the form of gifts or mutually beneficial economic exchanges in the virtual worlds (cf. Choo and Smith 2007, pp. 37, 49).

2.3.3 Integration

In the final stage of this money-laundering model, called the "integration stage" (or "dry cycle"), the white washed money, which by now appears to have been gained by lawful business activities, is reintegrated into the real economy (see Bülte 2006, p. 167; Jason-Lloyd 1997, p. 2).

So-called front companies[11] can be used for the integration of laundered money (cf. Hoyer and Klos 2001, p. 13) into the real economy, just as they are used to filter illegally obtained cash into the regular financial system in the first place. Front companies are apparently legitimate businesses – often in the hotel and catering sector, where cash transactions are common – whose financial records are inflated to create a false pedigree for the illicit money in the real economy. Other means include direct investments in real values, allocation of a loan, acquisition of companies, and simulated speculations (see Schneider et al. 2006, pp. 56f). Direct participation in the In-World economy provides yet another mechanism for integration.

2.4 Terrorism Financing

The already proven procedure for money-laundering described in the previous section is also suited for terrorism financing (in detail Solomon 2007). This has been explicitly pointed out by Gilles de Kerchove, the Counter-Terrorism Coordinator of the Council of the European Union (2008).[12] The danger is seen not only in

[11]Front companies can be used to conduct fraudulent international commercial trade to layer and integrate illegal proceeds (see Buchanan 2004, pp. 115, 118).

[12]Council of the European Union (11778/1/08 REV 1, p.6), Note from the Counter-Terrorism Coordinator: "Moreover, it is estimated that in 2006 over one billion USD was spent in goods and services in digital virtual communities (e.g. secondlife.com). As these communities may provide further layers of anonymity and profits can be transferred back to the real world, for example by electronic funds transfers, terrorist financing risks could emerge from the misuse of these websites."

the European Union, but also in the United States.[13] Although the model developed for money-laundering can be also used to illustrate the terrorism financing process, there is one overarching difference. In contrast to the money-laundering activities of criminal organizations, the funds involved in terrorism financing often come from legitimate money streams and get funneled into criminal enterprises rather than the other way around. Layering is not used for the washing of ill-gotten or "dirty" money, but rather to shield the origin of the money from public association with the recipient terrorist project.

3 Offences Committed Within the User-to-User Relationship

In order to understand the issue of criminal liability for offences committed by users of virtual worlds against their fellow users, it is necessary first to determine from whose perspective the virtual world actions are to be reviewed and to what extent the real users – as opposed to their virtual avatars – are to be considered either perpetrators or victims of criminal conduct. To this end, it is worthwhile to consider which term ("*virtual* crime" or "*virtureal crime*," *as I propose hereunder*) is more suitable for describing those crimes and their injurious effects, and to examine the legal meaning of the internal virtual world's rules. I will also examine two substantive areas of virtual or virtureal crimes: offences involving virtual assets and content offences such as virtual child pornography. The discussion of offences involving virtual assets will focus on the examples of fraud and blackmail, because the unstable system of appropriating assets in virtual worlds provides ideal opportunities for committing these offences. Content offences present special problems in the international arena because of the widely divergent legal standards of different countries. The discussion will highlight the example of virtual sexual interactions between adult-like avatars and childish looking avatars, for which offenders are currently facing vastly different criminal consequences under German law and U.S. law.

3.1 Determination of the Perspective

If we looked at virtual world actions from the point of view of a user who moves in these virtual worlds (In-World perspective),[14] our experience would be comparable

[13]See United States Department of State: Bureau for International Narcotics and Law Enforcement Affairs (2009, p. 6): "Observers also fear that terrorist groups may use virtual worlds to meet, chat, plan activities, and perhaps transfer funds. The added venue and jurisdictional challenges of following virtual money and value trails in and out of the virtual world compound the challenges regulatory and law enforcement agencies already face in the real world."

[14]Cf. Kerr (2008, p. 5), who distinguishes "between virtual and physical perspectives".

to taking a trip to a society ruled by the proverbial "law of the jungle."[15] An inhabitant can injure or liquidate another – under circumstances that would constitute actionable bodily harm or manslaughter or even murder in the real world – with complete impunity. Consider the example of the 43-year-old piano teacher *Mayumi Tomari*. She met the man of her dreams in the popular Japanese online game *MapleStory* and "married" him purely digitally within that world. However, after some time, this "husband" from the North-Japanese city of Sapporo, who was 10 years her junior, suddenly separated from her. For revenge, she liquidated him – the virtual version of him. She then penetrated into his on-line account, deleted his user profile and wiped out his existence in the *MapleStory world*. This case caused quite a stir in the online community, the trail of which can still be found under the keyword "virtual murder" (see Kölling 2008; Emigh 2008; Excite DigiWeb 2008).

Another example is an auction of avatars as slaves. If these had been human beings instead of avatars, the elements of human-trafficking[16] and/or unlawful imprisonment[17] would certainly be fulfilled.

Of course, a virtual-world avatar is not a "person" that can suffer an injury any more than it can inflict one. The erasing of an avatar is neither a murder nor manslaughter; an auction of an avatar is no trafficking in human beings; virtual rape is no rape because no human person is physically violated. An avatar is not human being, but only the digital representation of a fictional persona assumed by a person in a virtual world. It concerns merely the visual depiction of a physical injury, homicide, or rape (similar Kerr 2008, p. 6).

To have legal meaning in the real world, virtual-world activities have to be assessed from the real-world perspective, in terms of whether a real person suffered an injury that was caused by the deliberate action of another real person, or – in cases where crimes against property is alleged – whether the alleged crime resulted in the loss of an asset with real value. The causation standard – commonly employed in criminal law – should be based on the link between the last human action and the resulting injury. As such, virtual-world activities cannot give rise to liability for those criminal offences that by definition involve physical harm to a human person (e.g., murder, manslaughter, assault, battery, torture, rape, slavery, or human trafficking) or for those crimes that involve materiality (e.g., theft and unlawful appropriation under German law).

Likewise, a computer generated avatar – regardless of the software steering him – has no legal personhood.[18] Hence, it cannot be held accountable for the real-world

---

[15]Or, (in the concept of the idealistic philosophy) it could be described as the relapse from the civil society in the natural state.

[16]In Germany punishable according to Sect. 232ff. German Criminal Code (StGB).

[17]In Germany punishable according to Sect. 239 StGB.

[18]Cf. the thought experiment of *Ralph Kosters* "Declaration of the Rights of Avatars" (printed in Duranske 2008, pp. 351f; also Lastoska and Hunter 2004, pp. 63f): this idea may be absurd at first sight, however, it is not so new. Since some time, it has already thought whether a computer system and in particular an autonomous (intelligent) electronic agent should have a legal

effects of its "actions" in a virtual world (cf. Cornelius 2002, pp. 353, 354; Habel 2008, pp. 71, 76).[19] This lack of accountability is proper at least so long as an avatar is steered by a single user who controls its every movement[20] and the origin of the avatar's actions can thus be consistently attributed to a single human actor.[21] The action of the human user is decisive for the purposes of civil law effectiveness of "stretched" declaration of intention (based on the notion of task sharing between person and machine) (see Cornelius 2002, pp. 353, 355). Only the human activity is crucial for the responsibility under criminal law.

As argued above, actions that have consequences only in the virtual world have no rational meaning in the context of criminal liability. Rather, criminal liability can potentially arise only where a user's virtual-world activities have effects that can be observed in the real world by external observers. Therefore, rather than the term *virtual crime* – which is often used to describe criminal offences which are recognizable within the virtual worlds (cf. Brenner 2001, p. 1; Howell 2004, p. 103; Kerr 2005, p. 197; Lastoska and Hunter 2004, p. 293; Williams 2006), the term *virtureal crime* is hereinafter used to emphasize the primacy of real-world consequences in the very concept of criminal liability and to preclude any suggestion of criminal liability for those activities whose effects are exclusively virtual or In-World.

3.2 Legal Meaning of the Internal Virtual World's Rules

Let us look again at the virtual world's actions – the erasing of an inhabitant of a virtual world – from the point of view of an objective third party who never enters the virtual world. If this erasing is executed with means available in the relevant platform and according to the internal rules of the virtual world, this behavior has no criminal consequences. On the contrary, this act could even be considered as fulfilling a purpose immanent to the game (as for example, acts of violence in *World*

personality or not; (see supporting documents at Cornelius 2002, pp. 353, 354; cf. also Andrade et al. 2004, 84ff.; Weitzenboeck 2001, pp. 204, 211).

[19]As far as can be seen this is valid not only for the German legal system (Hettenbach 2008, pp. 217, 221). From civil law view, the proposal was developed to intruduce the *Electronic Person* as a new legal institute (see Wettig and Zehender 2003; cf. also the statement of Wiebe 2006, p. 80): "Electronic agents could be established in this respect as a third category beside natural and legal entities."

[20]This condition is fulfilled (up to now) with the avatars in virtual worlds (cf. van Kokswijk 2008, pp. 207, 212).

[21]Lastoska and Hunter (2004) speak in this context about a *Cyborg* (p. 64), (see also van Kokswijk 2007, p. 146): "Avatars, the user-controlled entities that interact with virtual worlds, are a persistent extension of their human users, and users identify with them so closely that the human-avatar being can be thought of as a cyborg."

of Warcraft).[22] The same holds true for the conquest of virtual territories or the abstraction of a virtual resource. If this happens according to the rules of the virtual world and within the functionalities available in its environment – as designed (without tampering) – then, of course, the question of criminal liability does not arise. Thus, the issue is considered here only as it relates to circumstances wherein a perpetrator manipulates either the technological framework (e.g., operating software) of the virtual environment or the victim's will by inappropriate measures like deceit or force.

The idea that such internal rules as game rules should also be decisive in the legal assessment of participants' behavior is not new. Like sports tournaments and other competitive franchises, the internal rules of a virtual world configure its content and establish the courses of action, all of which give a virtual world its character and distinguish it from other virtual worlds. Ideally, rules also guarantee to all users the same chances of participation. This is vitally important in cases where there is a matter of determining a winner (such as sweepstakes, sports tournaments, and play fights). The purpose of such game rules is to protect the players (active participants) and the viewers (passive participants) from threats to their life, health, and (real-world) assets that can arise from active or passive participation in the events (see Marburger 1982, p. 302).

The tendency of players to undergo a perspective change while engaged in a game is also not a new phenomenon. With regard to the interaction between law and game rules, *Andreas von Arnauld* has pointed out that the essential difference between the rules of a game and the rules of the real society is that the gamers intuitively try to escape from the "real reality" and move towards the construction of a "game reality" (see von Arnauld 2003, p. 33). The transition from one sphere of reality to the other tends to be seamless rather than clearly defined by strict boundaries. The rules governing the behavior of people making those transitions can be compared with a discussion about the legal meaning of *soft law*.[23] Strictly speaking, the rules of a game can have an effect only within the virtual platforms where they are established. To what extent the virtual worlds – which understand themselves, in the end, as a *community* of actors – can be regulated well enough by self-given rules and where there is a need for compelling limits by law, is a question that is still open and requires further discussion (cf. Lastoska and Hunter 2004).

[22]http://www.worldofwarcraft.com/info/basics/guide.html

[23]*Soft law* concerns principles, recommendations or codes of conduct whose non observance has no immediate legal consequences. The jurist differentiates law/non-law, however, puts the question to himself whether one should record documents without formal juridical binding effect as elements in the juridical system by an advanced understanding from > law<; (cf. to this discussion Zemanek 1998).

3.3 Offences Involving Virtual Assets

To determine whether certain virtual world activities amount to criminal offences such as fraud or blackmail, we must first ask whether the user suffers a real-world financial loss if control over a virtual object is taken away from him or her against the rules of the virtual world, assuming that the relevant virtual objects are properly allocated to his assets according to the rules. In a Dutch case of forced surrender of the masks and amulet, a punishment followed according to the theft regulations, because the primary argument was that the virtual objects that were stolen had a concrete value for the owner (see Maisch 2008).

3.3.1 Unstable Assignment of Virtual Assets

At first glance, the assignment of virtual assets to a user's accounts and/or the grant of certain copyrights to the user seem to provide adequate protection for the user's reasonable financial interests in his virtual possessions. But upon closer examination, it becomes apparent that, in practice, such assignments are not so unequivocally favorable to the assignee. Often, providers of virtual worlds partially negate any rights of the users in the virtual objects. For instance, *Linden Lab*, it its Terms of Service, grants users copyrights in the virtual objects that they create In-World, but then effectively takes it all back in another section of the same Terms of Service by extracting a guarantee from users that *Linden Lab* would have:

> "... the perpetual and irrevocable right to delete any or all of your Content from Linden Lab's servers and from the Service, whether intentionally or unintentionally, and for any reason or no reason, without any liability of any kind to you or any other party" (available at TOS, Second Life and Duranske 2008, pp. 297f).

According to Sect. 3.3 of the *Terms of Service (*TOS, Second Life), the user has to agree that the account and all data located there are the property of *Linden Lab* regardless of existing copyrights. Furthermore, *Linden Lab* shall have the right to close the account without compensation for the user,[24] at any time and for any reason.[25] *Linden Lab*'s terms are not at all unusual, but quite in keeping with the general terms and conditions of other providers. *Blizzard,* as the provider of *World*

[24]In Sect. 2.6 of the *Terms of service* is written: "Linden Lab may suspend or terminate your account at any time, without refund or obligation to you"; see Duranske 2008, p. 305.

[25]See Sect. 5.3 of the *Terms of service* "All data on Linden Lab's servers are subject to deletion, alteration or transfer. When using the Service, you may accumulate Content, Currency, objects, items, scripts, equipment, or other value or status indicators that reside as data on Linden Lab's servers. THESE DATA, AND ANY OTHERDATA, ACCOUNT HISTORY AND ACCOUNT NAMES RESIDING ON LINDEN LAB'S SERVERS, MAY BE DELETED, ALTERED, MOVED OR TRANSFERRED AT ANY TIME FOR ANY REASON IN LINDEN LAB'S SOLE DISCRETION"; see Duranske 2008, pp. 312f.

of Warcraft, reserves all rights with regard to ownership and property for itself[26] including the right to delete an account at any time for any reason.[27] *MindArk* as the provider of the virtual world *Entropia Universe*, in its *End User License Agreement*, reserves the right to delete an account without respecting any claims of compensation.[28]

If those contract terms are really legally enforceable, the provider can delete the account (for any reason or no reason) and remove the user's control over the virtual objects assigned to him or her, without legal remedy or claims for compensation. For the purposes of this paper, it is assumed that such terms are enforceable and this assumption is hereinafter referred to as the "Working Hypothesis."

This would mean that the user has actual access and control of the virtual objects assigned to his or her account only *as long as* the provider does not use its actual power (and perhaps legally enforceable right) to close or delete the user's account. This asset would be assigned to him only temporarily and could be taken away from him or her without his or her consent at any time. This tenuous and transient nature of the user's actual, exercisable rights over his or her virtual assets may mean that such assets do not rise to the status of legally protected assets, and consequently, another user could take them away without facing any consequences by criminal law.

3.3.2 Limits of the Legal Protection of Assets

What are the limits of the legal protection accorded to a user's assets? To approach the answer to that question, we must first look to other recognized areas of German criminal law, such as expectancies and endangerment of assets and illegal possession, each of which has been problematic with regard to the legal protection of assets (cf. Hefendehl 2006, Sect. 263 marginal number 534; Schünemann 2005, Sect. 266 marginal number 134) (Fig. 1).

---

[26]See the *Terms of Use Agreement*: "No Ownership Rights in Account. NOTWITHSTANDING ANYTHING TO THE CONTRARY HEREIN, YOU ACKNOWLEDGE AND AGREE THAT YOU SHALL HAVE NO OWNERSHIP OR OTHER PROPERTY INTEREST IN THE ACCOUNT, AND YOU FURTHER ACKNOWLEDGE AND AGREE THAT ALL RIGHTS IN AND TO THE ACCOUNT ARE AND SHALL FOREVER BE OWNED BY AND INURE TO THE BENEFIT OF BLIZZARD." (Available at World of Warcraft® 2011, TOS).

[27]See the *Terms of Use Agreement*: "Account Suspension / Deletion. BLIZZARD MAY SUSPEND, TERMINATE, MODIFY, OR DELETE ACCOUNTS AT ANY TIME FOR ANY REASON OR FOR NO REASON, WITH OR WITHOUT NOTICE TO YOU." (Available at World of Warcraft® 2011, TOS).

[28]See Sect. 3: "Participant Account . . . MindArk and its affiliates reserve the right, at their sole discretion, to refuse approval of an Account, to refuse access to an Account, to terminate an Account and to remove, edit or add content, without notice." and sect. 6: "Account Inactivity and Account Termination [. . .] In the event that your Account is locked or terminated, no refund will be granted." (Printed in Duranske 2008, pp. 337, 340).

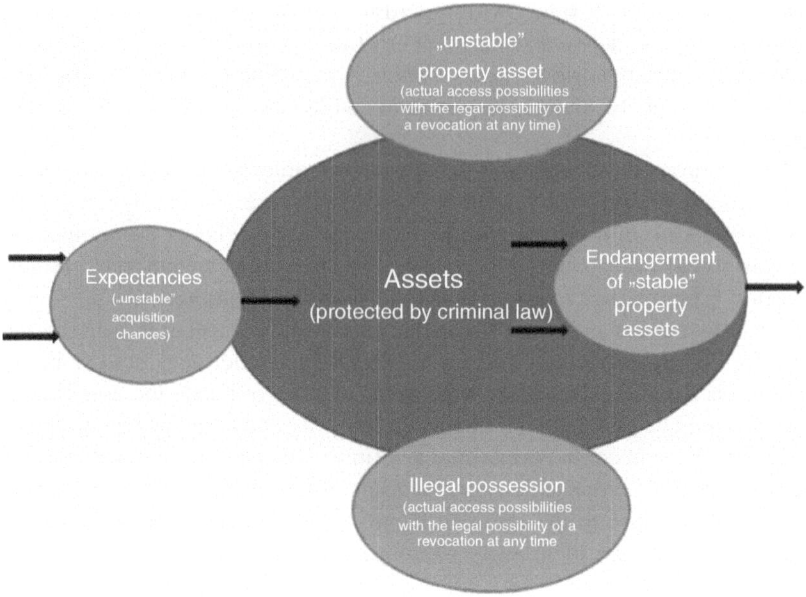

Fig. 1 Assets protected by German criminal law

In the case of expectancies, it is debatable whether the mere chance to acquire an asset already carries with it an economic value. In the context of endangerment of property, it is the threat that is debatable while the financial value of the assets might be well established and stable. The question is whether the mere endangerment of a stable property asset (assigned to the assets of the victim and protected by law) is already an existing financial loss, even if the chance of actual loss is remote (cf. Hefendehl 2006, Sect. 263 marginal number 532). The endangerment of property assets and actual financial loss can be thought of as a continuum, which moves in the direction of a substantive financial outcome: either profit or loss (see Hefendehl 1994, p. 23).

Illegal possession is yet another good point of comparison for analyzing the status of unstable property assets, because it provides a model for the tension between the rights of the actual possessor (the one who has access to and the ability to dispose of the object) and the rights of the lawful owner, where the possessor has a legal obligation to pass the object to the lawful owner on demand.

(a) "Unstable" property assets and endangerment of "stable" property assets

An argument for drawing a parallel between the "unstable" property asset of virtual objects and the endangerment of "stable" property assets is that in both cases, the assets have a concrete value to the user/owner. The virtual-world user has used his own, "real" money or manpower to acquire the virtual objects. These objects have a concrete value in use for him as well as a current market value which he or she can realize at his or her own discretion, assuming the provider does not delete his account. However, the principles developed for the endangerment of "stable" property assets deal with the fact that there is not an effective, substantial decrease of the property assets already available (see Hefendehl 1994, p. 23; cf. also Pröll 1919 pp. 124, 148f). This does not reflect the exact problem discussed here, since it does not involve the danger of a loss, but rather a loss that has really occurred – the removal of virtual objects. Moreover, the relevant preliminary question of whether these virtual objects are properly considered to be the legally protected assets of the user is simply not addressed in the context of endangerment, which deals with a specific set of issues involving "stable" property assets, whose current ownership status is not in question.

(b) "Unstable" property assets and expectancies

It seems natural to compare the "unstable" nature of virtual property assets to expectancies, as both are transient interests in property. The holder of the expectancy tries to receive the asset finally "in his pocket" (see Hefendehl 2002, p. 190). He or she would like to remove the uncertainly in the probability of acquisition and receive the property's full, present value. The frustration of this final acquisition because of the interference of a third party can be seen as a relevant financial loss (see Hefendehl 2002, p. 190).

Similarly, the "unstable" property asset existing in a user's virtual world account can be taken away any time without compensation by the service provider. One advantage that the present owner of an unstable property asset has over the expectant owner of a stable asset is that, unlike the expectant owner, the present owner may – where possible – sell or trade the asset for value, thus removing the uncertainty or "instability" from his property right. He or she can convert the virtual goods – his "unstable" property assets – into "real" money (e.g., by selling it on a commercial platform such as *eBay*) as long as this possibility is not first annulled by the provider exercising its power to delete the user's account at any time.

The parallels between expectancies and unstable property assets are limited, however. Expectancies with actual chances of acquisition are seen only as property assets if they are based on a sound legal basis and allow the holder the power to develop the full right (cf. Wessels and Hillenkamp 2010, marginal number 535). Likewise, unstable property assets can be stabilized only if the user is able to convert the unstable financial situation by a trouble-free development into a stable financial situation at any time. But this is not generally true in the virtual world context, at least not under the Working Hypothesis, which assumes the provider has an enforceable right to unilaterally delete the account of the user without compensation at any time.

Another distinction between expectancies and unstable property interests in virtual objects is that virtual objects represent – whether they are sold or not – a concrete resource for the user. He or she can use it as a tool to enrich his or her virtual existence. The personal avatar becomes stronger and mightier or just more aesthetically pleasing, and with it he or she can satisfy his or her demands from the virtual world. For this, he or she may already have used economic values (such as real money or manpower), coming from his or her real, legal estate. These virtual objects have – regardless of the question of a later economic gain – not only a current market value, but also a concrete value in use for the user. Because of this value, the user may even prefer to retain the virtual object and to attempt to stabilize his or her ownership of it rather than exchanging it for money. By contrast, an expectancy, regardless of the market value of the expected asset, usually offers the beneficiary no present utility value. The expectant owner normally tries to convert the expectancy into a full right and to stabilize his or financial interest in it. These differences between expectancies and unstable property assets militate against constructing the legal treatment of the two types of interest in precisely the same manner.

(c) Unstable property assets and illegal possession

Finally, another point of comparison exists that may provide an analytical framework for the legal status of unstable property assets: the question of whether illegal possession of property can give rise to a legally recognizable property interest. The parallels are found in the *provisional nature* of the legal right and in the exercise of *actual control* of the asset.

The provisional nature of the illegal possessor's right means that he or she must immediately relinquish the possession if it is claimed by the legal owner or other lawful possessor. Nevertheless, he or she is protected by the German civil law against an unlawful interference with his or her possession (verbotene Eigenmacht)[29] by unauthorized third parties. Apart from the economic value of actual possession and control, the fact of the possession itself confers a legal assignment, although only a weak one, which is effective against another unlawful trespasser but is ineffective against a beneficiary with a superior legal claim. The possession in an article of property that is protected by civil law (regardless of actual ownership) is also protected by criminal law (Prevailing opinion see BGH 2008; Lackner and Kühl 2007, Sect. 263 marginal number 34; Tiedemann 2005, Sect. 263 marginal number 140; Wessels and Hillenkamp 2010, marginal number 535; with references to other opinions Küper 2008, pp. 370f). Consequently, the user of a virtual world who has actual control over the virtual goods assigned to his or her account, but whose rights are provisional, can invoke these rights against third parties under the criminal laws (cf. Habel 2008, pp. 71, 75f; Klickermann 2007, p. 766, 768; Trump and Wedemeyer 2006, pp. 397f), but they are ineffective against the provider's "superior rights" (which include, according to the Working Hypothesis, the absolute right to delete the account without compensation to the user). As such, a user's property rights in the virtual goods in his or her properly assigned account – although subject to abrogation at any time, as presumed here – are protected by criminal law.

[29]Sect. 859ff. of the German Civil Code.

3.3.3 Applicability of Criminal Liability to Losses of Unstable Property Assets

The criminal assessment of the financial loss represented by a user's loss of a virtual asset does not depend on whether the asset is stable (i.e., not subject to the provider's unilateral right to the delete the user's account without compensation) or unstable (subject to the user's absolute rights). The virtual goods associated with the user's account, over which he or she has the power of disposition – even if that power is subject to abrogation by the provider – are components of the user's property interest in the account. A deprivation of this property interest by a third party without corresponding compensation results in a financial loss for the user and gives rise to possible charges of fraud or blackmailing.

3.4 Content Offences

In virtual worlds, special attention is paid to those offences that involve insult, defamation, inciting of violence, glorification of power over others, and pornographic content. The criminal laws define the elements of a crime to place explicit restraints on the freedom of individuals to engage in certain kinds of behavior, which reflect the values and moral standards of a society. To meet the limited extent of this paper, the present discussion will focus on the example of *Sexual Ageplay,* a role-playing game mostly between adults, in which contacts with sexual content are carried out between adult-looking and childish-looking avatars.[30] This example is especially salient because of the vastly different criminal law treatment of this kind of behavior under German Law on the one hand and American Law on the other hand.

3.4.1 German Law

In German Criminal Law, pornography that depicts even purely fictive representations of children is prohibited, under Sect. 184b paragraph 1 German Criminal Code (see Cornelius 2011, marginal number 309; Fischer 2011, Sect. 184b marginal number 5; Gercke and Brunst 2009, marginal number 322; Sieber and Nolde 2009, p. 11). This is because the policy behind banning the distribution of pornography is to prevent the encroachment of the sexual development of youngsters, and it is presumed that such encroachment can be caused by the images themselves, regardless of whether they depict a real or fictional event

[30]Thus, the broadcast "Report Mainz" from the 7th of May, 2007 uncovered facts with virtual sex between childishly and adultly looking avatars.

(cf. Hilgendorf et al. 2005, marginal number 394f). The virtual game *Sexual Ageplay* falls squarely in this category of prohibited material.

3.4.2 American Law

(a) Child pornography prevention act

The Child Pornography Prevention Act (CPPA) of 1996 prohibited

> any visual depiction, including any photograph, film, video, picture, or computer or computer-generated image or picture ... that ... is, or appears to be, of a minor engaging in sexually explicit conduct ... (Codified as 18. United States Code (U.S.C.) 2000, Sect. 2256 (8); see also Kornegay 2006, pp. 2129, 2140; Malamuth and Huppin 2007, pp. 773, 774; Duhaime 2009, pp. 347, 349).

According to the *CPPA*, participating in the *Sexual Ageplay* would be punishable as a crime. However, the United States Supreme Court struck down that *CPPA* provision in *Ashcroft* vs. *Free Speech Coalition (*Ashcroft, 535 United States Report (U.S.) 2002, 234), holding that the provision is overbroad and unconstitutional, as far as it forbids the production of entirely virtual images, which bears no relationship to the statute's purpose of protecting children from exploitation in the context of pornographic performances. The court pointed out that the *CPPA* had forbidden something "that records no crime and creates no victims by its production" and that "virtual child pornography is not 'intrinsically related' to the sexual abuse of children." (Ashcroft, 535 U.S. 2002, 234, 236; see also Duhaime 2009, pp. 347, 349; Kornegay 2006, pp. 2129, 2140).

The Court also rejected the Government's claim that virtual child pornography can indirectly cause harm by creating "some unquantified potential for subsequent criminal acts" (Ashcroft, 535 U.S. 2002, 234, 250) and added:

"The mere tendency of speech to encourage unlawful acts is not a sufficient reason for banning it. The government' cannot constitutionally premise legislation on the desirability of controlling a person's private thoughts.' Stanley v. Georgia, 394 U.S. 557, 566 (1969)." (Ashcroft, 535 U.S. 2002, 234, 253).

(b) Prosecutorial remedies and other tools to end the exploitation of children today act

The Congress (the American legislature) responded to *Ashcroft v. Free Speech Coalition* with a piece of legislation called the *Prosecutorial Remedies and Other tools to End the Exploitation of Children Today Act* (PROTECT Act). The PROTECT Act attempts to meet, at least formalistically, the Supreme Court's constitutional objections to the CPPA language struck down by the *Ashcroft* decision. In the new formulation, the phrase "appears to be" was replaced with "indistinguishable from," (Malamuth and Huppin 2007, pp. 773, 783) so that "child pornography" is now defined as "any visual depiction" of minors engaging in sexual conduct, ... including where "such visual depiction is a digital image, computer image, or computer-generated image that is, or is indistinguishable from, that of a minor engaging in sexually explicit conduct" (18 U.S.C. Sect. 2256 (8)(B)).

The term "*indistinguishable from*" is reasonably read to apply to images that are not possible for a normal viewer to discern from an image of a real child. The phrase "*appears to be*" included a broader range of images, including those that resemble the external appearance of a child to some indeterminate degree of accuracy. The "indistinguishable from" standard supposes that a reasonable person would not be able to perceive a difference, whereas the "appears to be" language suggested that one can but need not perceive a difference (cf. Kornegay 2006, pp. 2129; 2150f). The revised definition of child pornography expressly excludes such representations that are "drawings, cartoons, sculptures, or paintings depicting minors or adults" (18 U.S.C. Sect. 2256 (11)). However, while this new, narrower formulation might answer the Supreme Court's concern that the prior legislation had been overbroad in its reach, it does not appear to meet the Court's charge that the symbolic speech banned by the legislation does not actually harm any real children. Unless such harm is shown, the Court is unlikely to find that sexual depiction of fictional children, even if "indistinguishable" from real children in appearance rises to a serious enough governmental objective so as to trump the constitutional guarantee of free speech. Therefore, sexual images of childish looking avatars and games such as *Sexual Ageplay* would probably not be criminalized as child-pornography in the United States, because the PROTECT Act, to the extent that it tries to ban such images and games, would probably not survive a review by the Supreme Court.

4 Conclusion

This paper has attempted to show through examples that the current state of the German criminal law is largely adaptable enough to fight new threats of criminal activity appearing through the use of virtual worlds. Unless appropriate measures are taken early, it can be assumed that virtual worlds will be used increasingly for money-laundering and terrorism financing, due to the easy and almost cost-neutral manner in which money can be manipulated and their true sources can be obscured by exchanging real money for virtual values.

There are significant gaps in the protection available under the criminal law with regard to losses of virtual goods, because currently, no clear legal standards exist for ascertaining the real value associated with such virtual goods. In cases where the loss of virtual goods is caused by swindle or force, the German criminal law provides protection even where only unstable property assets are concerned.

Finally, intercultural differences factor into the analysis because of the global nature of virtual world participation. The difference becomes clear in particular with content offences. While fictional child pornography – such as *Sexual Ageplay* in virtual worlds – is punishable under German law, the same material may well be protected by the fundamental constitutional guarantee of freedom of speech in the

United States. Such differences call for the creation of certain minimum international standards with which to regulate certain activities, which have already raised criminal law issues in the "normal" Internet, and whose potential for serving criminal purposes has grown significantly in the context of virtual worlds.

References

Andrade F, Novais P, Neves J (2004) Issues on intelligent electronic agents and legal relations issues. In: Cevenini C (ed) The Proceedings of the LEA 2004 – workshop on the law of electronic agents, Rome, pp 81–94

Ashcroft v. Free Speech Coalition (2002) Cases adjudged in the Supreme Court at October term, 2001. United States Reports, 535. http://www.supremecourt.gov/opinions/boundvolumes/535bv.pdf, accessed on 20 June, 2011

Bell MW (2008) Toward a definition of "Virtual worlds". J Virtual Worlds Res 1. http://journals.tdl.org/jvwr/article/viewFile/283/237, accessed on 20 June, 2011

BGH (1972) Zur Kunstschutzfähigkeit eines Vasenleuchters. Gewerblicher Rechtschutz Urheberrecht 1:38–39

BGH (1995) Zur Frage der Urheberrechtsschutzfähigkeit von Schmuck (hier: Silberdistel-Ohrclip) als Werk der angewandten Kunst im Sinne von § URHG § 2 Abs. URHG § 2 Absatz 1 Nr. 4 UrhG. Gewerblicher Rechtschutz Urheberrecht 8(9):581–582

BGH (2008) Verlust der Diebesbeute als Vermögensschaden. Neue Z Strafrecht 11:627

Boyd G, Moersfelder M (2007) Global business in the metaverse: money laundering and securities fraud. SciTech Lawyer 3:4–7

Brenner S (2001) Is there such a thing as "virtual crime"? Calif Crim Law Rev 1:4 http://www.boalt.org/CCLR/v4/v4brenner.htm, accessed on 20 June, 2011

Buchanan B (2004) Money laundering – a global obstacle. Res Int Bus Finance 18:115–127

Büchner T (2008) Die urheberrechtliche Schutzfähigkeit virtueller Güter. Kommunikation Recht:425–428

Bülte J (2006) Die Geldwäschegesetzgebung als Ermächtigungsgrundlage für den Informationsaustausch zwischen den Steuerbehörden und den Strafverfolgungsorganen: . . . der §§ 30 IV, 370a AO, 261 StGB, 10, 11 GwG. Peter Lang Verlag, Frankfurt a.M

Chaikin D (1991) Money laundering as a supranational crime: an investigatory perspective (clone). In: Esser A, Lagodny O (eds) Principles and procedures for a new transnational criminal law. Max-Planck Institut für ausländisches und internationales Strafrecht, Freiburg

Choo K-K, Smith RG (2007) Criminal exploitation of online systems by organised crime groups. Asian Criminol 3:37–59

Cornelius K (2002) Vertragsabschluss durch autonome elektronische Agenten. Multimedia Recht 6:353–358

Cornelius K (2011) Besonderheiten des Strafrechts und Strafprozessrechts in der Informationstechnologie. In: Leupold A, Glossner S (eds) Münchener Anwalts Handbuch IT-Recht. C.H. Beck, München

Council of the European Union (2008) Revised strategy on terrorist financing. http://register.consilium.europa.eu/pdf/en/08/st11/st11778-re01.en08.pdf, accessed on 20 June, 2011

Dreyer G, Kotthoff J, Meckel A (2004) Urheberrecht. C.F. Müller Verlag, Heidelberg

Duhaime G (2009) Criminal law – expert testimony not required to distinguish pornographic images of real children from virtual children – United States v. Wilder. Suffolk Univ Law Rev 42:347–352

Duranske B (2008) Virtual Law: navigating the legal landscape of virtual worlds. American Bar Association, Chicago

Düsseldorf OLG (2008) Freie Benutzung eines Bronzeengels gemäß § URHG § 24 UrhG. Z Urheber Medienrecht 2:140–143

Emigh J (2008) Online gamer arrested for 'virtual murder' in Japan. http://www.betanews.com/article/Online-gamer-arrested-for-virtual-murder-in-Japan/1224888499, accessed on 20 June, 2011

Excite DigiWeb (2008) Japan: Virtueller Mord mit Folgen in der Realität. http://digiweb.excite.de/japan-virtueller-mord-mit-folgen-in-der-realitat-N2205.html, accessed on 20 June, 2011

European Network and Information Security Agency (2008) Virtual worlds, real money. Security and privacy in massively-multiplayer online games and social and corporate virtual worlds. http://www.enisa.europa.eu/act/it/oar/massively-multiplayer-online-games-and-social-and-corporate-virtual-worlds/security-and-privacy-in-virtual-worlds-and-gaming/at_download/fullReport, accessed on 20 June, 2011

Fischer T (2011) Strafgesetzbuch – StGB: und Nebengesetze. C.H. Beck, München

Geis I, Geis E (2007) Rechtsaspekte des virtuellen Lebens. Erste Ansätze zur Konfliktlösung in Second Life. Comput Recht 11:721–725

Gercke M, Brunst PW (2009) Praxishandbuch Internetstrafrecht. Kohlhammer, Stuttgart

Habel OM (2008) Eine Welt ist nicht genug – Virtuelle Welten im Rechtsleben. Multimed Recht 2:71–77

Hartmann M (2007) Markenfälschungen überschwemmen Second Life. http://www.tecchannel.de/news/themen/business/481267/markenfaelschungen_ueberschwemmen_second_life/, accessed on 20 June, 2011

Hefendehl R (1994) Vermögensgefährdung und Exspektanzen: Das vom Zivilrecht konstituierte und vom Bilanzrecht konkretisierte Herrschaftsprinzip als Grundlage des strafrechtlichen Vermögensbegriffs. Duncker & Humblot, Berlin

Hefendehl R (2002) Vermögensgefährdung und Exspektanzen als Prüfsteine eines normativ-ökonomischen Vermögensbegriffs. In: Schünemann B (ed) Die Stellung des Betrugs im Strafrechtssystem. Centaurus Velag, Pfaffenweiler, pp 185–248

Hefendehl R (2006) Münchner Kommentar zum Strafgesetzbuch. §§ 263-358 StGB, §§ 1-8, 105, 106 JGG. C.H. Beck, München

Hettenbach D (2008) Das Übereinkommen der Vereinten Nationen über die Verwendung elektronischer Mitteilungen bei internationalen Verträgen. Mohr Siebeck, Tübingen

Hilgendorf E, Frank T, Valerius B (2005) Computer- und Internetstrafrecht. Ein Grundriss. Springer, Berlin

Hoeren T (2010) Neue Medien. In: Loewenheim U (ed) Handbuch des Urheberrechts. C.H. Beck, München

Howell BA (2004) Real world problems of virtual crime. Yale J Law Technol 7:103–122. http://www.yjolt.org/files/howell-7-YJOLT-103.pdf, accessed on 20 June, 2011

Hoyer P, Klos J (2001) Regelungen zur Bekämpfung der Geldwäsche und ihre Anwendung in der Praxis. Verlag Erich Schmidt, Bielefeld

International Monetary Fund (2010) World Economic Database. http://imf.org/external/pubs/ft/weo/2009/02/weodata/index.aspx, accessed on 20 June, 2011

Jason-Lloyd L (1997) The law on money-laundering: statutes and commentary. Frank Cass Publishers, London

Kern C (1993) Geldwäsche und organisierte Kriminalität. Dissertation, Regensburg

Kerr O (2005) Virtual crime, virtual deterrence: a skeptical view of self-help, architecture, and civil-liability. J Law Econ Policy 1:197–214

Kerr O (2008) Criminal law in virtual worlds. University of Chicago Legal Forum, Forthcoming; GWU Law School Public Law Research Paper, p 391

Klickermann PH (2007) Virtuelle Welten ohne Rechstansprüche? Multimed Recht 12:766–769

Koch P (2006) Die rechtliche Bewertung virtueller Gegenständen auf Online-Plattformen. http://www.jurpc.de/aufsatz/20060057.htm, accessed on 20 June, 2011

Kölling M (2008) Virtuelle Gewalt vor Gericht. http://www.heise.de/tr/blog/artikel/Virtuelle Gewalt-vor-Gericht-272014.html, accessed on 20 June, 2011

Köln LG (2008) Virtueller dom in second life. Multimed Recht 8:556–559
Kornegay J (2006) Protecting our children and the constitution: an analysis of the "virtual" child pornography provisions of the Protect Act of 2003. William Mary Law Rev 47:2129–2167
Küper W (2008) Strafrecht. Besonderer Teil. Definitionen mit Erläuterungen. C.F.Möller Vlg., Heidelberg
KZero (2010) Virtual goods: good for business? http://www.kzero.co.uk/blog/?p=3624, accessed on 20 June, 2011
Lackner K, Kühl K (2007) Strafgesetzbuch (StGB): Kommentar mit Erläuterungen. Beck Juristischer Verlag, München
Lastoska G, Hunter D (2004) The laws of the virtual worlds. Calif Law Rev 92:1
Lehdonvirta V (2008) Real-money trade of virtual assets: new strategies for virtual world operators. http://www.hiit.fi/~vlehdonv/documents/Lehdonvirta-2008-RMT-Strategies.pdf, accessed on 20 June, 2011
Maisch MM (2008) Niederlande: "Diebstahl" virtueller Gegenstände ist strafbar. http://www.rehmoblog.de/?p=894, accessed on 20 June, 2011
Malamuth N, Huppin M (2007) Drawing the line on virtual child pornography: bringing the law in line with the research evidence. NY Univ Rev Law Soc Change 31:773–827
Marburger P (1982) Die Regeln der Technik im Recht. Heymann-Verlag, Köln
Nänni M (2008) Der Vertrag über die Nutzung virtueller Welten. Jusletter. http://www.rwi.uzh.ch/lehreforschung/alphabetisch/vdc/cont/Jusletter_MN.pdf, accessed on 20 June, 2011
Nänni M (2009) Märkte virtueller Welten. Schultheiss Verlag, Zürich
Pröll R (1919) Gewinnvereitelung, Vermögensgefährdung und Vollstreckungsabwendung. Eine Untersuchung über die Vermögensbeschädigung beim strafbaren Betrug. In: Kohler J (ed) Archiv für Strafrecht und Strafprozess, vol 66. R v Decker's Verlag, Berlin, pp 124–197
Psczolla J-P (2008) Onlinespielrecht. Rechtsfragen im Zusammenhang mit Onlinespielen und virtuellen Parallelwelten. Tectum Verlag, Marburg
Report Mainz ARD (2007) Internetspiele. Tummelplatz für Kinderpornografie. http://www.swr.de/report/-/id=233454/nid=233454/did=2060062/1h0wega/index.html, accessed on 20 June, 2011
Rippert S, Weimer K (2007) Rechtsbeziehungen in der virtuellen Welt. Zeitschrift für Urheber-Medienrecht:272–281
Schneider F, Dreer E, Riegler W (2006). Geldwäsche. Formen, Akteure, Größenordnung – und warum die Politik machtlos ist. Gabler, Wiesbaden
Schulze G (2004) Abschnitt 2. Das Werk. In: Dreier T, Schulze G (eds) Urheberrechtsgesetz. C.H. Beck, München
Schünemann B (2005) Strafgesetzbuch. Leipziger Kommentar. §§ 264-302: BD 7. De Gruyter, Berlin
Sieber U, Nolde M (2009) Sperrverfügungen im Internet. Nationale Rechtsdurchsetzung im globalen Cyberspace? Duncker & Humblot, Berlin
Solomon J (2007) Trends in terror finance. http://www.c-cft.org/publication/index.html, accessed on 20 June, 2011
Stessens G (2000) Money laundering: a new international Law enforcement model (Cambridge studies in international and comparative law). Cambridge University press, Cambridge
Tiedemann K (2005) Strafgesetzbuch. Leipziger Kommentar: §§ 223-263a: BD 6. de Gruyter, Berlin
Trump S, Wedemeyer H (2006) Zur rechtlichen Problematik des Handels mit Gegenständen aus Onlinecomputerspielen – "Stinkt" Geld etwa doch? Kommunikation Recht 9:397–404
United States Department of State: Bureau for International Narcotics and Law Enforcement Affairs (2009). International Narcotics Control Strategy Report – Volume II: Money Laundering and Financial Crimes. http://www.state.gov/p/inl/rls/nrcrpt/2009/vol2/pdf.TrendsinTerror FinancePart2.pdf, accessed on 20 June, 2011
US Presidents Commission on Organized Crime/United States (1984) Cash Connection: Organized Crime, Financial Institutions, and Money Laundering. Interim report to the President and the Attorney General

van Kokswijk J (2007) Digital ego – bad ISBN: social and legal aspects of virtual identity. Eburon, Delft

van Kokswijk J (2008) Granting personality to a virtual identity. Int J Hum Soc Sci. http://www.waset.org/journals/ijhss/v2/v2-3-37.pdf, accessed on 20 June, 2011

Virtual World News (2009) Virtual worlds popularity spikes. http://www.virtualworldsnews.com/2009/07/virtual-world-popularity-spikes.html, accessed on 20 June, 2011

von Arnauld A (2003) Normativität von Spielregeln. In: von Arnauld A (ed) Recht und Spielregeln. Mohr Siebeck, Tübingen

von Heintschel-Heinegg B (2010) Strafgesetzbuch (StGB). C.H. Beck, München

Wandtke A-A, Bullinger W, Block U (2009) Praxiskommentar zum Urheberrecht. C.H. Beck, München

Weitzenboeck E (2001) Electronic agencies and the formation of contracts. Int J Law Inf Technol 9:204–234

Wessels J, Hillenkamp T (2010) Strafrecht Besonderer Teil 2. Straftaten gegen Vermögenswerte. C.F.Müller Vlg., Heidelberg

Wettig S, Zehender E (2003) The electronic agent: a legal personality under German law. In: Oskamp A, Weitzenboeck E (eds) Proceedings of LEA 2003: the law and electronic agents. Unipub, Edinburgh, pp 97–113

Wiebe A (2006) Der Vertragsabschluss durch elektronische Agenten. In: Hoffmann M, Leible S, Sosnitza O (eds) Recht und Neue Medien Band 10. Vertrag und Haftung im E-Commerce. Boorberg, Stuttgart

Wieduwilt H (2008) Cheatbots in Onlinespielen – eine Urheberrechtsverletzung? Multimed Recht 11:715–719. http://www.telemedicus.info/uploads/MMR11-08-Wieduwilt.pdf, accessed on 20 June, 2011

Williams M (2006) Virtually criminal: crime, deviance and regulation online. Routledge, London

World of Warcraft® (2011) Terms of use agreement. http://us.blizzard.com/en-us/company/legal/wow_tou.html, accessed on 20 June, 2011

Xinhua (2009) China bars use of virtual money for real goods trading. http://www.chinadaily.com.cn/bizchina/2009-06/27/content_8330180.htm, accessed on 20 June, 2011

Zemanek K (1998) Is the term "soft law" convenient? In: Hafner G, Loibl G, Rest A, Sucharipa-Behrmann L, Zemanek K (eds) Liber Amicorum Professor Ignaz Seidl-Hohenveldern in Honour of his 80th Birthday. Brill Academic, Hague, pp 843–862

Index

K. Cornelius and D. Hermann (eds.), *Virtual Worlds and Criminality*,
DOI 10.1007/978-3-642-20823-2, © Springer-Verlag Berlin Heidelberg 2011

The manufacturer's authorised representative in the EU is Springer Nature Customer Service Centre GmbH, Europaplatz 3, 69115 Heidelberg, Germany. If you have any concerns regarding our products, please contact ProductSafety@springernature.com

Printed and bound by CPI Group (UK) Ltd, Croydon, CR0 4YY
01/10/2026
02225978-0018